D0299426

CONTENTS

PREFACE

Measurement is engineering. Engineering is the foundation of video, television, film and the cinema: in fact, everything to do with moving pictures. But many who work in the industry are not engineers. Many get caught up in a technology for which they are ill-equipped to deal. So where do these people begin? The intention of this small book—miniscule compared to the magnitude of the subject—set out to explore the system step by step, from bulb and battery, through early messaging, to first pictures, and on to where we are today.

A tall order. Yet seven years after the first drafts experimented with how to introduce video measurement to those who never expected to have the need to know, I am still being told: 'Take nothing out. Just keep adding to what's already there.' In that, of course, lies the essence of the subject: the principles are never obsolete. Pictures are pictures, the same whatever the means of their making, because they are the product of our creative intellect. So from first edition to third, nothing is cast aside, for everything has relevance to someone out there.

Good practices don't change, is another principle. By the same token the bad ones have to be gone over if they are to be laid to rest. A solid foundation is by its nature, hard work in the laying down, but no building will stand for long without it. Understand the basics, and the rest will follow. I try never to overwhelm the reader. This occasionally means side-stepping issues that may at times deflect us. Inevitably corners will get trimmed but, I hope, never cut. This book is an introduction. It makes no pretence to be anything else. It is aimed at newcomers to the industry and those already established who seek to broaden their horizons.

When considering the third edition, I was pressed for more of the practical questions posed in the second edition. Also, one aspect of the moving image—and one of considerable importance—had thus far been overlooked. It is audio. Since audio was used to develop an understanding of video, I thought it only fair to write a chapter specifically for it. Of course, having done so, one cannot avoid comparing the two: what applies to the one usually in some way applies to the other. And that helps both. The two have always been inextricably entwined, and together they strengthen our grasp of the whole. The change of title reflects the inclusion of audio.

As before, I thank old colleagues and friends, Peter Eggleston, John Kimberley, Steve Nunney, Wendy Ross, Keith Schofield and Martin Uren, and manufacturers Hamlet Video International and Leader Instruments who provided equipment. In particular I thank those who were cajoled into reading drafts.

Peter Hodges
September 2003

ACKNOWLEDGEMENTS

Artwork and photography is copyright of Peter Hodges. Illustrations of Hamlet equipment supplied by and used with the permission of Hamlet Video International Ltd.

INTRODUCTION

Why do we measure video?

Video is a high-tech business that makes use of engineering to acquire, store, manipulate, send and display pictures. Measurement is essential to engineering. To describe an engineering situation, we must be able to measure and quote all the dimensions. When we talk of pictures, which are the reason for video, it is insufficient to simply say 'it is too dark or too light'. These are photographic terms, perfectly legitimate where the esoterics of picture making are concerned, but they are not engineering parameters.

Engineering measurement makes sure all the parts fit. In video this means making sure the picture fits the system. Or, turning the argument around, making sure the system can handle the picture. Modern production techniques are always changing, bringing a constant pressure to alter and improve systems. Video engineering has standards set out in volumes published over many years: standards that are in daily use.

Video—we often hear—is easy. Just switch on and use. That's a fine ideal to aim for but it hides the vast amount of electronic processing taking place behind every shot, every programme, every network. Indeed, a great deal can be left to get along by itself, but some technical supervision must be on hand if errors are not to develop into faults and upset our carefully worked out schedules.

One cannot talk about measurement until it is clear what has to be measured. And this is not possible until the subject is properly understood. Consequently, we begin with the principles of electric signals, then through the video system, right up to digital video, dealing with the practical as well as theory. Measurement is the basis. Even more basic is the picture. This is never far away.

Knowledge is, by itself, not enough. Experience is the other vital commodity. No one can teach experience; it has to grow and expand in its own good time. A lot of experience has gone from the industry, either because it's too expensive or no longer thought necessary. Human presence can be engineered out of some areas, of that there is no doubt, but we have yet to reach the point where technology knows what the eye wants to see.

'It never fails' is another myth. No technology can provide that. Testing a piece of kit is no guarantee it won't fail as soon as your back is turned. This is no gloomy prospect, it's a fact of life, and one we have lived with for a very long time. This book sets out what has been known and used since electricity came to town. All that has been done is to turn it into a form that anyone with the will to learn can benefit from. To know and understand generates confidence.

This third edition includes the basics of audio to round out the story. And here again, as 'old video' persists, so do the roots of modern audio. Digital video and digital audio will always have their analogue base, alive and kicking within whatever new packaging is still to be invented. We wait to see where the technology will lead, but whatever the path, the analogue base will still be there. We see analogue, we hear analogue. Digits have their part to play in that.

Part One

The Foundation

CHAPTER 1

CIRCUITS AND SIGNALS

An electric signal is the sending of information by means of an electric circuit. Signals may take a variety of forms, they can be simple or complex, descriptions which change over time as technology develops. Today, audio may be described as a simple signal, yet where it is adapted to fit into, say, a mini-disc player it assumes a complexity far beyond that transmitted into our homes in the early days of wireless.

Video is a complex signal. In whatever form, video will always be complex. It must not only describe the picture but how it is constructed. To understand the video signal, we must go back to the beginning and look at the way a picture is converted into electricity for transmission. Understanding this requires some knowledge of electrical and electronic theory. However, the most onerous demands placed upon the reader will be to understand the philosophy behind signals, less so the maths and physics. So let's start right at the beginning with the simplest of electrical signals.

Sending signals

Take a simple circuit; that of a lamp powered by a battery. Figure 1.1 shows the battery and a lamp—a switch is also included to turn the lamp on and off. This is a two-wire circuit, one leaving the battery and one returning to it; at the lamp, there is one arriving and one leaving. The switch is placed in one of these wires—it doesn't matter which. Switch on and a current flows. Switch off and it stops. Figure 1.1 shows both sketch form and schematic form of this arrangement. It is conventional to use schematic diagrams with international symbols to describe a circuit, and we will follow this practice and add explanations as required.

There are many types of circuit, depending on what signal system is to be used and the kind of information it must carry. All have evolved from the battery, switch and lamp circuit. The switch may have gone, replaced by a more complex arrangement, the principle though, remains. And the sourcing, or sending, of the signal may originate with a two-wire circuit, and end at the destination with a similar two-wire circuit, but in between—the

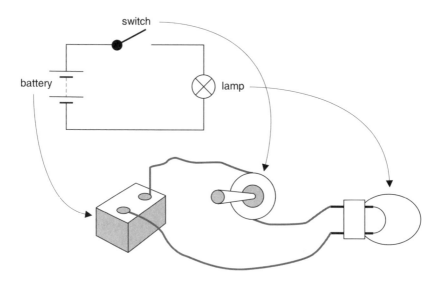

Figure 1.1a When the switch is closed the lamp lights. Closing the switch places the battery voltage across the lamp, driving a current through it. The lamp filament heats up and radiates light. This is a straightforward transfer of energy from electricity in the battery to heat and light. When used as a **signalling system**, the information transmitted is at its most basic for there are only two conditions: on or off.

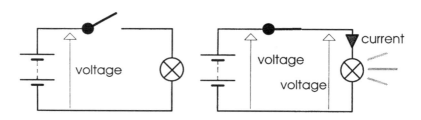

Figure 1.1b Two-wire electric circuit conditions. Measurement in this circuit is simple: we can measure the voltage and the current, and from these, know the whole of this circuit's values or parameters. Battery voltage is always present, but closing the switch effectively places the voltage across the lamp. The lamp forms a **load** on the battery voltage that causes a current to flow in the circuit. Battery energy is now transferred to the lamp, appearing as heat and light.

transmission system—we could meet any number of methods and media through which the signal passes, e.g. wireless, fibre link, or satellite.

Injecting a signal into a length of wire is like launching a missile. It can be aimed with proper regard for its size and shape, how far it has to travel and through what. Or, it can be hurled without thought for any of these. Our lamp and battery circuit would be in the latter category if just made up of bits of wire and insulating tape. Although able to signal on or off, its usefulness would be somewhat limited.

Even so, the comprehensive world-wide system of cable telegraphy created in the nineteenth century is based on this simple circuit. Using a battery and switch to send a signal or current along the cable or wire and a sensitive indicator to replace the inefficient lamp, messages in simple code are sent under the sea and over land. While the 'missile' here may be thought of as crude and the path it passes along little better, cables have now been in use for over 150 years, so proving the technique to be a remarkably reliable means of communication. Couple this to its inherent security and resistance to interference and it is easy to see how valuable the cable telegraph was to become in times of international stress. A point to reflect on with the rapid growth of today's hi-tech eavesdropping.

The complexity of signals as used in audio and video require greater sophistication in their handling and transmission than yesterday's cable tele-graph. In practice, the circuit is usually a fait accompli, often provided by a contractor. The actual line (as the cable is usually called) can be taken as conforming to a standard. The longer the line, of course, the more probable the chance of error or fault. Particularly so where the means of transmission changes from one system to another.

Comparing the circuit of battery, switch and lamp to a telegraph cable would be perfectly reasonable but the presence of a long interconnecting cable has to be considered. No cable or piece of wire is ever perfect. For short lengths, the metre or so of wire that makes up our basic lamp circuit, there is negligible effect on its operation. So simple a concept, however, starts to break down as the distance between the signal source and destination increases. In such a case, the connecting wire, whilst carrying the signal current, absorbs significant power from it.

Figure 1.2 shows a schematic diagram of the simple circuit extended into a cable, and the operation of sending a simple 'OFF–ON' type of signal. Also shown in graphical form is the effect of time from the point of switching on and launching the signal into the cable to the signal's appearance at the destination. The finite transmission time taken by an electric current to travel from source to destination, although very fast—approaching the velocity of light—the effect is significant in electrical terms over long distances.

Applying our battery voltage at the sending end of the cable, the first thing to happen is the cable 'starts to fill up with electricity'—a statement that simplifies the action but serves to illustrate the mechanism. The cable can, therefore, be said to have a capacity that must be filled before a signal can emerge at the far end. One can compare this to filling a pipe with fluid; quite a lot of fluid will go into a long pipe before any reaches the far end. But like all simple analogies, this one can be subject to misinterpretation, so avoid taking the idea too literally. It does, though, offer an alternative way to understanding in basic terms the concept of signal transmission over long distances.

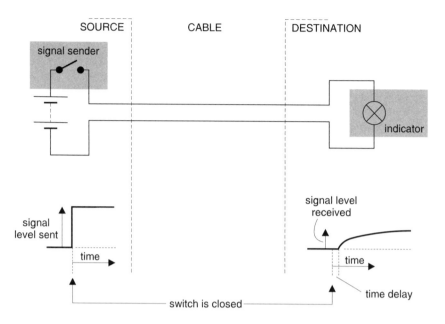

Figure 1.2   The simple circuit is extended into a cable. Note how the instantaneous rise of voltage at the source has become much slower when received at the destination. It has taken a finite time for the cable to 'fill up'. There is a time delay at the destination end resulting from the finite velocity of the signal travelling in the cable. This is the **propagation delay**. Some of the signal power has also been absorbed by the cable, resulting in a reduced signal level reaching the destination. This is the **signal attenuation**.

Source and destination

In an ideal world the signal appearing at the destination will be identical to that sent out from the source. From the discussion so far, we can see this ideal is not possible. Yet as long as the degree of degradation or attenuation is known and understood, correction can be applied and a practical and predictable signal communication system will be achievable. But what must we do to bring this about? This question is the bottom line of all signal transmission, so let us list the key requirements of a circuit:

1 The conditions, or characteristics, at the source and destination are known.
2 The circuit cable and associated equipment are compatible.
3 The circuit characteristics are known.
4 The signal and circuit are compatible.
5 The signal is able to carry the information required.
6 The signal will be immune from interference.

7 The circuit will be reliable.
8 The information will be secure.

Requirements 1 to 5 embrace the technical requirements of the circuit design. Requirements 6, 7 and 8 are largely dependent on the kind of circuit used and here, reference to 'circuit' may in practice, go beyond the two-wire circuit considered so far. It is quite usual over long distances to have combinations of cable, wireless, fibre optic, or satellite-based systems. But Requirement 1 states that the source and destination characteristics should be known. If we also know Requirement 3, which sets out the characteristics of the circuit, we can predict how the circuit will react to, and alter, the signal.

Receiving a signal

Figure 1.2 shows the signal distortion caused by the time element and cable capacity. Let us assume that the cable design is optimised for the job it has to do. Now the two most significant parameters of the cable are:

1 Cable resistivity: this causes signal power loss.
2 Cable capacity: how much electric current flows into it before the signal can appear at the destination.

The propagation delay of Figure 1.2 is the time taken for the signal to appear at the destination. A hundred years ago this was of no great significance, but now it most certainly is. Absolute time is now a universal requirement, and whatever the means of transmission, time differences must be considered. Cables may be used over kilometres or just centimetres. The length will inevitably have considerable effect on the signal and its distortion. All cables, whatever the length, will affect the signal to some degree, but by careful design this can be minimised and made predictable. Cable design influences, in particular, how effectively the signal is able to carry information, as well as how far and how quickly. This is the cable characteristic. An integral part of a cable characteristic is to state how the cable is loaded, or how the cable is terminated at the destination.

Terminating the cable

In the basic battery/lamp circuit, power is transferred from the battery to the lamp when the switch closes. How all this works was described years ago by Georg Ohm and his law is still the most universal in electric and electronic theory. Ohm's law states that a circuit—any circuit—has three elements:

1 **Voltage:** The battery produces a defined voltage based on its chemistry.

2 **Current:** The voltage drives an electric current into the load.
3 **Resistance:** The load offers resistance to the current and heats up in the process.

These three parameters are related by Ohm's law:

Voltage = Current × Resistance

All electric and electronic circuits possess these three elements and conform to this law. When current passes through the load it will heat up because power is dissipated in it. A signal is received as power; the power to operate a lamp or indicator. In more advanced circuits, this is the power to produce sound or pictures, usually with the aid of additional apparatus. Power cannot be sent unless there is a load, or resistance, to accept it. Power is dependent on the voltage applied and the current flowing in the load which is the product of the voltage and the current:

Power = Voltage × Current

The signal voltage can be present but no signal current will flow until a load is present. The destination load terminates the cable to complete the circuit. In the case of a long cable there will be a finite time before the load is 'seen' by the signal. The sending of power is, therefore, not possible at that instant the switch closes. Figure 1.3 shows this effect. If the cable characteristic and terminating load are correctly chosen, the cable itself will provide the correct

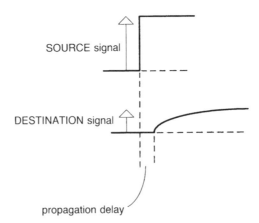

Figure 1.3   Propagation delay. The signal source is not immediately terminated by the destination load because of the propagation delay. For the signal to be launched properly, the design characteristic of the cable must provide the initial load so allowing the signal to enter the cable.

load for the signal at the source. The cable, source and destination are now said to be matched, allowing the signal to be sent with minimum loss and distortion. In practice the cable has to be correctly terminated at both ends, meaning that source and destination are required to match the characteristic of the cable.

The subject of cable termination will arise in later chapters for it is a very significant part of video transmission.

Creating a standard

A standard is created by common usage. The cable and termination characteristics described above are the standard for that particular circuit or transmission technique. In creating a transmission standard, we put in place the means to send and receive signals to and from any point that conforms to that standard. When proved and accepted, a standard will be promoted for the use of all. A standard enables interconnection, not only for long distance transmission, but also to connect one piece of equipment to another. Wherever the standard exists there is the means to interconnect. The value of this is obvious; system design is simplified and versatile and therefore cost effective.

The next important consideration is the ability to check out the system. The standard specifies all the parameters of the signal and the transmission circuit, including the cable and its termination. There are, however, many pitfalls for a signal en route from sender to receiver. We must ensure that the signal is generated accurately in the first case, and properly conforms to the standard. Signal measurement is central to this. Measurement is required at the source and at the destination, and the signal may undergo further checks, depending on how far it has to travel and by what method.

Now there is the means to guarantee that what is received is what the sender intends to be received.

However the measurement procedure is carried out it must be disciplined. It may be strict, following a regulated practice, for instance, each time a circuit is used. Or it may be less formal, where all that is required is confirmation from the destination that the signal is being received. Whichever is most appropriate will depend upon:

1 How often the circuit is used.
2 The length of the circuit, or total transmission path.
3 How many stages there are in the route.
4 How prone the signal is to distortion or degradation.
5 Whether or not the circuit is one of proven reliability.
6 The importance of the information sent.

The first and second points are easy to evaluate. A short length of cable will not require the attention devoted to an international circuit, and if it is regularly used its reliability will be known. Point 3 is related to the second, the greater the complexity, the more attention will be required. Point 4 is often dependent on length and complexity, but is a measurable quantity. Point 5 raises the spectre of failure, and an unreliable system should be checked regularly and thoroughly. Here, it's experience that counts. The final point can only be evaluated by the users ... programme originator and customer, not the operator or contractor. The distinction is important.

The standard offers protection against the inevitable errors that will crop up in any practical system. The signal is measured at source, defined as being within the standard system limits, and sent on its way. Upon its arrival a similar check is made to verify that it has arrived with minimum degradation, and is therefore accepted. Sender is happy. Recipient is happy. As would be the operator who set up the circuit. Here lies the fundamental reason to measure; to know that what is sent is correct and agree that what is received is likewise correct.

The integrity of the standard must at all times be upheld if reliable and consistent signal transmission is to be accomplished. It is an obligation on all users to see that this is so, and the system is not allowed to fall into disrepute.

Cable and wireless circuits

Figure 1.4 shows how a circuit with more than one transmission medium may be developed from the basic two-wire cable in Figure 1.2. The important principle here is that while both source and destination conform to the same standard, neither sender nor receiver need know the characteristics of the rest of the circuit. In this case, the source feeds a radio link, and the destination is fed from the same link. The radio link will have its own standard, its own parameters. But at its input it will comply with the source standard, and its output to the destination standard. The wireless transmitter will convert to a standard of its own to supply the signal to the antenna. At the far end, exactly the same applies, the receiver takes the signal from its antenna and converts to the standard the destination requires.

Using the principle of standard interconnections, the system now lends itself to analysis by test and measurement. The set-up can be used to check the accuracy of sender and indicator. Simply connect them together at (A) and (B). Although these may in practice be some undefined distance apart, it is reasonable to assume that an identical receiver be available at the source for just that purpose; test and measurement. Of course, such a method demands the two receivers are identical, at least as regards point (B). But that is what the standard does; it defines the characteristics of the equipment at the points of interconnection. Figure 1.5 does this: the indicator is directly connected to the sender. Both sender and indicator conform to the standard in that they are interconnectable.

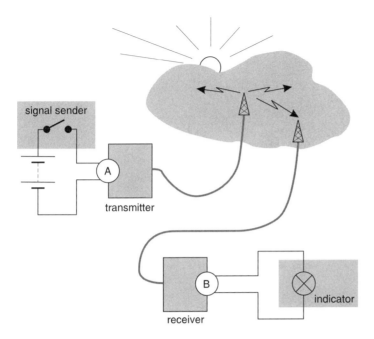

Figure 1.4   The wireless circuit. Here is a simple transmission circuit, it may be intercontinental or simply from inside a sports stadium to the truck outside. But note how the sender and indicator no longer 'look' into a long length of cable. At Point (A) there is now a transmitter. This effectively separates the 'outside world' from the sender. Likewise at Point (B) there is a receiver isolating the indicator. Both these devices, of course, serve the primary function of transmitting and receiving, via their antennae. The characteristics of terminals (A) and (B) can now conform to a standard, making them have the same characteristic, and we are back to our original two-wire circuit as regards the circuit seen by both sender and indicator.

Cables and wireless antennae need specific equipment to operate them. A cable requires a line driver, whilst a wireless transmitter will drive an antenna. The destination will require a line receiver or a wireless receiver. And our simple cable circuit in Figure 1.2 has developed into a more universal one.

A standard becomes established when operators recognise it as a successful one, encouraging its use and expansion. Eventually all equipment and systems fall into line and base their interconnections on that standard. A whole range of options may now be made available for different operations.

As has already been shown in Figure 1.4, a complete transmission system may be a combination of techniques or media. We have seen that the presence of a circuit at the source does not necessarily mean a cable travelling all the way to the destination. It is only the standard at source and destination that

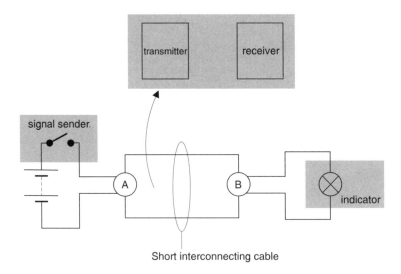

Figure 1.5 The test set-up of sender and indicator. This test set-up shown may be exchanged for other equipment that is designed to the same standard. The circuit is therefore easily adapted for other purposes.

must be the same if signal accuracy is to be guaranteed. To send anywhere, whether to the other side of the globe, or just to the room next door, can now be undertaken with the confidence of knowing that what we send will arrive as we expect it to.

Where next?

So far we have considered only a signal based on a battery and a switch as the sender, and an indicator of some kind. More complex signals, such as audio and video, use the same principles, but the additional complexity of these signals places new demands on the circuit that require new standards. Such is the complex nature of audio and video that errors may be many, significant or otherwise, a fact of life only put into its rightful place by the discipline of test and measurement. But as before, once established, a standard must always remain true.

But what of our battery, switch, lamp, and bits of wire? It is very easy to dismiss this as ancient technology and long past its sell-by date. Not quite. There is a very close relationship between what was part of the nineteenth century and what is now the twenty-first. Digital techniques: the principle of noughts and ones—OFF and ON, just as our switch turned the lamp ON, then turned it OFF again. Digital video is nothing more than 'ones' and 'noughts' ... a signal that is either on or off. Yet there remains the old,

old problem of what the eye sees and the ear hears. Cable telegraphy and digital technology are only transmission—with today the added value of storage and processing—and nothing to do with our human senses.

But our battery, switch and lamp have shown us a little of the future, and that for the moment must be sufficient.

CHAPTER 2

TIME AND THE COMPLEX SIGNAL

We have mentioned the complex signal, and have taken note that video falls into this category. Let us now see how this comes about, and what it means to the transmission and measurement of such signals and the standards involved.

The more complex the signal, the more stringent is the process of sending. Generally speaking as the rate of information increases then so do the demands on the circuit. How do we define 'information rate'? Return again to cable telegraphy based on the battery and lamp circuit. Here, the rate is the operator's speed in converting the information into a code based on an on/off signal, followed by the reader's speed in decoding. The code used is Morse code and is much slower than speech ... very much slower.

Speeding up the transmission of cable telegraphy is feasible. First, we must replace the human operator with a faster automatic system of switching, then redesign the circuit to function at the higher rate and finally, install a high-speed reader at the destination. This may all seem very logical, but if the information is speech-based it obviously makes more sense to send speech as it is; a sound or audio signal. Hence the Bell telephone system captured the enthusiasm of our forebears. High-speed data transmission, which is what an automatic rapid on/off system really is, was not introduced until teleprinter and facsimile systems appeared later.

Speech was never going to be an easy proposition, particularly over long distances with nineteenth-century technology. Audio is more prone to distortion and interference than on/off signals ... another hint to the great digital upheaval to come. Speech is analogue. On/off is digital.

However, in those long gone days, from where so much of our engineering springs, the idea of speech transmission was so attractive that a very great deal of effort went into developing the means to make it possible. The result was 'telecommunications' as we know it today.

Video is a relative newcomer. Nonetheless, the ready-made base was there; audio research had provided the essential elements of telecommunication engineering, and video inherited these. Not least was the nomenclature, or how the various components came to be described. We will, therefore, divert

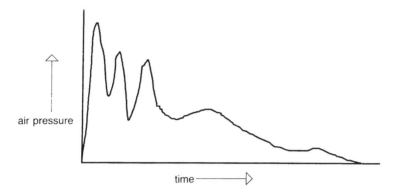

air pressure

time ⟶

Figure 2.1   A typical sound wave pattern. A mechanical crashing sound, similar to a hammer striking a solid object, produces an air pressure variation like this. It is this variation of pressure that is heard.

our attention to sound to see how audio signals help explain why video is where it is now.

Figure 2.1 shows a typical sound wave in graphical form. It begins as a sharp increase in air pressure followed by a slower decay. The shape, or 'waveform' as it is called, is of a noise that could be a crash of some sort, possibly a hammer blow on a solid object. Note how irregular the shape is. Every such event will have its own distinctive form, and is sometimes called a 'sound signature'. It is so irregular that however many times the event is repeated, the waveform will never be exactly replicated.

Whilst the waveform in Figure 2.1 would be heard as a crash, the waveform in Figure 2.2 is quite the opposite. This will be heard as a pure, steady tone. Where the first example has a start and a finish, the second is continuous. Figure 2.2 describes a sine wave and represents the purest form of sound. The simple motion of a pendulum is the classic mechanical sine wave, also known as simple harmonic motion. Sine waves are not confined to mechanical systems, they are fundamental to electrical circuitry as well. They appear in air, or fluid movement, where they are often known as 'waves'. Sound waves, sea waves, not forgetting the ubiquitous radio waves that travel via the so-called ether.

Figure 2.2 is of a sine wave signal, and is represented by a graph that shows signal level and time just as in Figure 2.1. But it is a continuous signal . . . there is neither beginning nor end. The graph has no axes, or reference scales, and nor are there units. Only the arrows indicate the direction of increase of magnitude.

The measurement of pure tone is easy because it doesn't change. Speech changes all the time; from silence to a shout. Therefore, speech must be measured constantly if we are to avoid exceeding the standard laid down for our circuit or not to make full use of it.

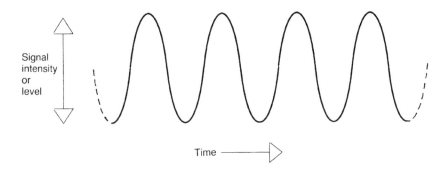

Signal
intensity
or
level

Time

Figure 2.2 A sound waveform of pure tone. A sine wave does not change shape, it is continuous. Defined thus, without change, it would theoretically continue forever. Note that the vertical scale of 'signal intensity' has a double-ended arrow indicating a variation around a mean value.

Before we can measure we must assign units. There are two. Magnitude and time. The latter is inextricably linked to information rate, in simple audio it's how fast we speak and the kinds of sounds we make. And before we measure we must also have a scale for the units. Magnitude, in electronic terms is 'amplitude' or 'level'. Where audio is concerned, amplitude refers to practical, constantly varying signals, while level is used for steady state signals. For our purposes, either may be used. The actual measurement is of 'voltage'. Time is always measured in seconds or fractions thereof.

All this may seem academic but where the more complex waveforms of video are considered, these principles are fundamental to a thorough understanding of the subject.

In Figure 2.3 there are three sine waves. They are all related, their start times coincide, as do their levels, at point (A) and all return again to the same level at (B). From (B) the process repeats. The sine waves differ in only one respect: their frequency. Frequency describes how many times per second the sine wave repeats itself, or completes one cycle. The lowest frequency wave completes one cycle from (A) to (B). Another completes two cycles and the highest frequency wave completes four cycles, all within the same time.

Frequency is specified in cycles per second. The term 'cycles per second' is now superseded by 'Hertz', abbreviated to 'Hz', after the German physicist who first identified radio waves. One Hertz is one cycle per second, which is written as '1 Hz'.

The representation of three distinct waves in Figure 2.3 is a theoretical situation. Sound pressure—air pressure on our ear drums—can have only one value at any particular point in space and instant in time. Therefore the three add together. As also will signals launched into a common circuit. Three signals may be produced, but when brought together they will combine into a single one … add mathematically to produce a more complex wave.

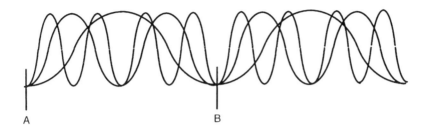

Figure 2.3 Three related sine waves. Each has a frequency that is a multiple of the others.

The resulting waveform of the three sine waves is not sinusoidal and appears as in Figure 2.4. The resultant no longer has the symmetry of the sine wave, or the constancy, nor has it the equality of swing either side of the horizontal, or 'time', axis. Although one can see a relationship with each individual component, for instance, the signal repeats itself at the same rate as the lowest frequency wave. In fact the resultant has a band of frequencies spanning from the lowest to the highest frequency sine wave. We call this 'bandwidth'. The resultant signal is therefore precisely related to the three originals. Reversing the logic, we can take the resultant, dismantle it, and recover the originals.

Applying the same logic to Figure 2.1 it is possible to analyse the sound of a crash. Yet to build, or synthesise, such a signal requires a very complex combination of sine waves. The theory, however, quite clearly states that this is possible and, indeed signal synthesisers are a common feature of audio practice. In fact Figure 2.1 does not truly represent what actually takes place. The sudden pressure increase is followed by a decay. If, however, we were to continue the observation, we would see the pressure reverse for, like a wave on water, a flow in one direction will slow down and eventually reverse. This is an oscillating system. Oscillating mechanical and electrical systems

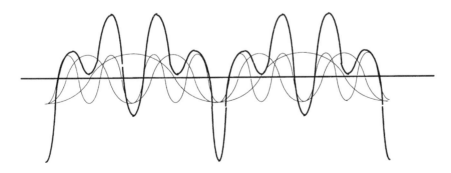

Figure 2.4 The three sine waves in Figure 2.3 added together. Adding together sine waves produces a sine-based resultant whose variations either side of the mean are not always symmetrical.

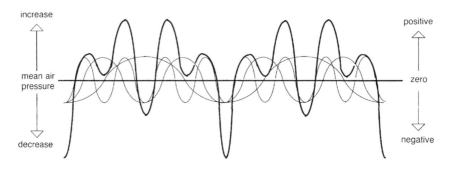

Figure 2.5   Defining the values of the axes. Two scales are shown for the vertical axis. The left-hand one is air pressure about a mean value. On the right-hand side the mean value has been subtracted. The pressure variations may now be considered as positive and negative of the horizontal axis. Note that the 'time' axis is not shown, it is often assumed but not stated, unless the time scale is relevant.

will swing from one side to the other as long as energy remains in them to continue. Eventually, the energy will be used up and the system will become stable once more at the mean.

Figure 2.5 shows a vertical axis scale has been added with a reference line above which the pressure rises, and vice versa. This translates into positive and negative values of the signal; positive above the reference line and negative below. The reference line now becomes, by definition, zero level. In sound pressure terms, the line represents normal air pressure about which the signal swings, but it is usually more convenient to ignore this offset, referring to the signal as swinging positive and negative about this value

Converting to an electric signal

The acoustic signal, on conversion into its electrical equivalent, produces a varying voltage of similar shape. Figure 2.6 has no units specified for amplitude and as (from Ohm's law) voltage and current are proportional, either may be assumed. Voltage has become the established convention to express level or amplitude of signals. But remember, when considering voltage as the unit we must never lose sight of the fact that it is the signal current that carries the information. Either a steady direct current, as in telegraphy, or the fluctuating speech signal in audio. But both are subject to the relationship of voltage, current and load resistance.

Figure 2.6 is a complex signal. If the values of its component frequencies were stated as being between 20 cycles per second and 20 000 cycles per second, it would describe a signal of the highest audio standard. This is the frequency band of human hearing. Therefore, the frequency range of hi-fi audio is often stated as being 20 Hz to 20 000 Hz (slightly different

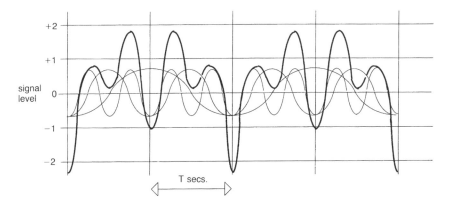

Figure 2.6 Defining the values of the axes. Placing a scale of values against a waveform enables it to be measured. Here the signal level is scaled from +2 to –2, called 'amplitude'. T is a value in seconds between the horizontal spaces, as time is continuous, no start or finish is stated.

values may be sometimes substituted but these need not concern us here). As far as the ear is concerned, the sound in Figure 2.1 can be represented by a combination of sine waves whose frequencies will lie between 20 and 20 000 Hz.

When audio is converted into an electrical signal it may be described as alternating current. A battery can only deliver a signal that is a direct current, i.e. it always flows in one direction as determined by its chemistry. Thus it has a polarity indicated as positive and negative. Direct current has two units; current expressed in amps, and volts (the force driving the current). Alternating current also uses the same units of amps and volts, but, as we have seen, there is the added parameter of frequency to consider. Frequency may be stated as the rate at which the polarity alternates.

Therefore a signal based on an alternating current has two parameters that may be used to carry information: voltage and frequency.

With voltage we can state a scale of level from, say, zero to 1 volt. This is quite arbitrary; there is no reason why designers cannot use any other set of values to suit their own individual requirements. Inside equipment, on the other side of the connectors, any value of voltage may be present, the choice is entirely the designer's. It is only where the signal enters and re-emerges again that we need be interested in actual values of signal level, for this is where it must comply with the standard.

The concept of time

The original starting point of time is now a very long while ago and so we must establish our own points of reference from which events may be measured. For instance, we can make a reference at which a particular event in the signal takes place, this may be stated as: t = 0 s. (The standard unit of time is the second.) Figure 2.7 shows a time axis, a single horizontal line marked out with a scale of seconds. The reference from which the measurement is made is where t is zero. The two significant events are the door opening and the person speaking.

t =   −1   0   1   2   3   4   5   seconds

Figure 2.7   The timed sequence. A door into a room opens, a person enters, walks to a lectern and starts speaking. At a particular point in time the door opens and a stop watch, or clock, is started. When the person speaks, the watch is stopped and the time noted as 5 seconds. This describes the complete sequence of events that may be written as:

START: At t = 0 seconds   Door opens
                          t = +1 second   Door closes

From t = +1 second to t = +4 seconds   Person walking to lectern

                          t = +4 seconds   Person reaches lectern
FINISH: t = +5 seconds   Person speaks

Our simple illustration has more in it than at first thought necessary. The time scale has only to cover five seconds yet it begins at minus one and runs over by a second. It's like telling a story: we need a little background to understand the whole. Where there is a sequence it is often useful to see extra at both ends to satisfy ourselves that there's sufficient to understand the whole and nothing of significance exists just outside. The importance of this will become apparent as we proceed.

Figure 2.8 is of a sine wave with the same time scale as in Figure 2.7. It shows four cycles. These too, may be described as events, but because they are repetitive the term 'cycle' is more appropriate. Of the four cycles shown, three are within the time scale, and from this we are able to determine the frequency. Frequency, f, is defined as the number of cycles per second, so:

$$f = \frac{3 \text{ (no. of cycles)}}{5 \text{ (seconds)}} = 0.6 \text{ cycles/second} = 0.6 \text{ Hz}$$

Now return to the basic battery and lamp circuit that started it all, here now shown in Figure 2.9. Compare this to Figure 2.1 and note the similarity. Graph (C) has a similar rapid increase in level at t seconds. The same analysis may also be made of Figure 2.9 as was made of Figure 2.1 regarding its relationship to harmonic motion and the sine wave. Exactly the same analysis may be applied to Graph (A). The battery produces a steady voltage, there is no variation, cyclic or otherwise. The battery voltage is said therefore to have a frequency equal to zero.

This is a very significant point to make; the lowest limit of frequency has been determined, that of a direct current. The upper limit does not exist in practical terms for it is only reached at infinity. In our ideal circuit the voltage rise is instantaneous on closure of the switch. The voltage step so produced is unrealisable for it implies infinite rate of change, requiring an

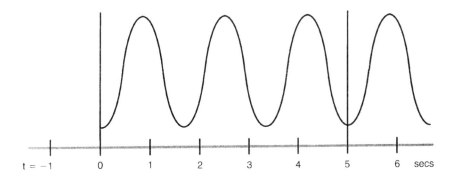

Figure 2.8 Adding a time scale to a sine wave. The time scale is not absolute, zero seconds being placed arbitrarily on a negative half cycle. The scale allows the time taken for subsequent cycles to be read off.

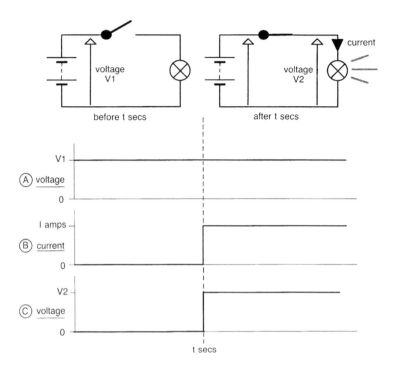

Figure 2.9   Timed sequence of a switched lamp and battery circuit.
Graph (A) shows the battery voltage as a constant value V1. When the switch
closes at time t seconds, V1 appears across the lamp. Graph (B) shows
the current increasing from zero to that drawn by the lamp after t seconds.
Graph (C) is the voltage V2 across the lamp. Note that after t seconds, V2
increases to equal V1.

infinite range of sine wave frequencies to do so. In practice this is limited by
bandwidth.

Bandwidth

The principle of bandwidth is fundamental to the understanding of how
audio and video are sent from one point to another. The effects of bandwidth
are far reaching.

   To observe the true effect we must first magnify the part of the waveform
at the t seconds point as in Figure 2.10. Two features emerge. First, the actual
rise commences after t seconds . . . the actual point of switch closure. Second,
the shape of the rise. Note how this appears to follow a sine waveform from
zero to maximum. Figure 2.11 illustrates the mechanism of how this comes
about.

   From all this we can determine the bandwidth of the signal. The voltage rise only appears to be instantaneous, in practice, let's say it takes a

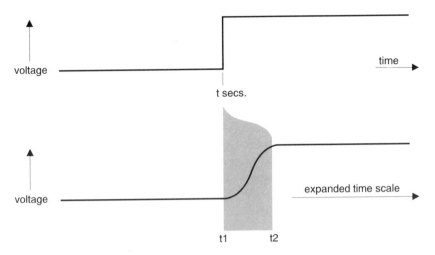

Figure 2.10 Magnifying the event. The increase of voltage at t seconds is shown expanded, and taking the finite time t1 to t2 to complete the transition. This is the **rise time** of the event. Note how the expanded scale means an observation over a much shorter period.

two-millionths of a second, which is half a microsecond, usually written as 0.5 μs. Before and after t seconds the waveform is a constant voltage (actual value is here not important), which is DC, or zero frequency, the lower bandwidth value. The transition takes 0.5 μs, which is equivalent to a sine wave

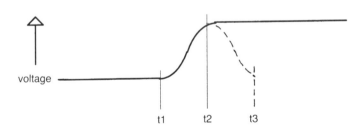

Figure 2.11 The sine form of the voltage rise. How the part sine wave shown in Figure 2.10 is used to determine the upper bandwidth point. From t1 to t2 is a half cycle. Extrapolate to t3 will complete the cycle. Therefore, the sine wave period, or wave length, is t1 to t3.

t3 – t1 = λ seconds, where λ is the wavelength of the sine wave

Frequency of the sine wave, $f = \dfrac{1}{\lambda \text{ s}}$ Hz

of period 1 μs, and a frequency of:

$$\text{Frequency } f = \frac{1}{1.0\ \mu s} = 1\,000\,000 \text{ Hz or } 1.0 \text{ MHz}$$

The lower bandwidth point is 0 (the frequency of DC). The upper bandwidth point is 1 MHz. Therefore, the bandwidth $= 1 - 0 = 1$ MHz.

In practice, the shape of voltage changes, such as shown in Figure 2.13, are rarely perfectly sinusoidal, there are many other influences to upset so simple a model. It does, however, provide a useful picture of how a practical complex waveform is built up and how it may be dismantled again to analyse. And it is worthwhile to reflect back to Chapter 1 and Figures 1.2 and 1.3. Those of academic bent might feel inclined to consider the connection . . .

Of all the various signals considered so far, that of direct current (DC) and the single sine wave, or pure tone, are special cases for each consists of only one frequency. All others are combinations of sine waves of various frequencies and levels. Audio, as already stated, has a frequency range of 20 Hz to 20 000 Hz, which define the limits of the audio band.

$$\text{Audio bandwidth} = 20\,000\text{--}20 \text{ Hz} = 19\,980 \text{ Hz or } 19.98 \text{ kHz}$$

As frequencies of a very wide distribution are being considered, now is a good time to look at abbreviations. Cycles per second have been given the term 'Hertz' which has already been abbreviated to 'Hz'. To this may be added a whole series of prefixes to simplify the expression of large numbers. Frequencies over 1000 Hz are usually abbreviated to kilohertz (kHz). As 19.98 kHz is so close to 20 kHz, the audio bandwidth is usually approximated to 20 kHz.

Intelligible speech can be transmitted using a considerably smaller bandwidth than 20 kHz. 'Telephone quality', as it is called, typically has band limits of 300 Hz and 3400 Hz, which is a bandwidth of 3.1 kHz.

At this point, it is worth looking at sending more than one signal down a cable simultaneously. The telephone system established a very simple principle, as is shown in Figure 2.12. The two microphone signals travel round the circuit, carried on the current set up by the battery, and each heard by both parties (the all-important side-tone where each person hears their own voice). Together, the signals occupy a total bandwidth of 3.1 kHz. At first sight, the idea of two similar signals in the same circuit implies twice the bandwidth. Not in this case. The two people have a single conversation . . . their signals are combined into one. Add another, and another . . . as many as you want, and there is still one conversation, merged to hubbub no doubt, but one signal nonetheless.

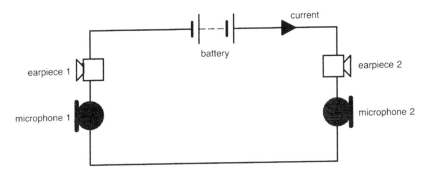

Figure 2.12 The basic telephone circuit. A two-wire circuit with battery. Sender and destination are identical and interchangeable, each with microphone and earpiece. The battery sends a current around the circuit that is modulated by the sound waves impinging on both microphones. As the current also passes through the earpieces, each person hears the other, plus their own voice as well.

Where secrecy is required, then this simple circuit falls down, for the signals are not isolated from each other. Overhearing or interference of one signal by another can only be eliminated when each signal has its own circuit, or channel.

A channel is a block of bandwidth allocated to a signal. A circuit can be devised to accept more than one channel, and hence carry more than one signal. Providing more channels requires increasing the bandwidth. For instance, two independent channels of speech will require two lots of 3.1 kHz each when combined, or encoded, into one signal for sending over a single circuit. Such a circuit would require a total bandwidth of 6.2 kHz, and gives an indication of how information and bandwidth are interrelated.

The bandwidth figures, as stated above, do not, in themselves, state the actual frequency limits of the circuit concerned. For instance, one or more audio channels, each with a bandwidth of 3.1 kHz, could be placed anywhere in the whole frequency spectrum. Figure 2.13 shows six channels, each with 3 kHz of bandwidth coded together onto a carrier signal with its own frequency of 1 MHz.

The carrier and its six channels would be a much more complex signal than a single channel of 3 kHz. Its bandwidth points to this fact; it is six times that of one channel. However, 18 kHz occupies only 1.8 per cent of the spectrum at an operating frequency of 1 MHz, revealing how, by using higher and higher frequency carriers, more space becomes available to individual signal channels. The principle of using one circuit for more than one signal is known as multiplexing, and is the basis of modern telecommunications, whether for telephone, broadcasting, Internet, or whatever.

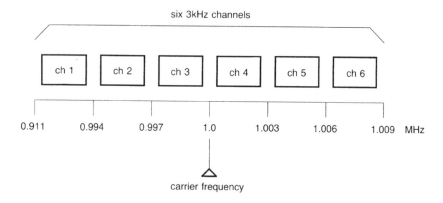

Figure 2.13   Multichannel operation using a single circuit. The bandwidth of the whole signal is from 0.991 MHz to 1.009 MHz, which is 0.018 MHz or 18 kHz (3 kHz each channel). 6 × 3 kHz = 18 kHz.

So there's a choice. If we want to send more information in a given time, we either increase the number of circuits or the bandwidth. Both cost money, but the multiplexed single circuit usually wins.

How about digitising?

To see how digital telecoms perform, we once again go back to earlier times, and the battery, switch and lamp of Figure 1.1. The Bell telephone system sent speech over a two-wire circuit, but its limitations were serious. Over long distances attenuation, or signal losses, placed soft talkers at a disadvantage, as it also did for those who spoke with an unfamiliar accent or had a speech impediment. Take all these individuals, convert their messages to simple 'ons' and 'offs', then send as code, and all these problems disappear. What we've done is converted analogue to digital.

The code also lends itself very well to accept more channels. And we can prune the circuit into the bargain because on/off is much more easily detected than a distant voice will be heard. Add a degree of intelligence (a computer with appropriate software) and we can make the source and destination 'talk' ... discuss problems with the code, seek 'best guess' answers for the decode and check whether it's correct or not. The cable and its many links can degrade quite a lot now and still bring the far side of the world right into the room where you're sitting.

Such technology wasn't available to Bell, of course, but people still wanted to talk ...

Consider this ...

The timed sequence in Figure 2.7 can now be seen rather differently. The whole sequence runs for 5 seconds, and in that time there's a given amount of information.

However, let's ask the man to sprint to the lectern. . . take only 2.5 seconds. Now, is the amount of information the same or not? Of course it's only half the amount. We know that because, if we record the event it will occupy only half the space—2.5 seconds of tape, or half the chunk of memory if it's loaded into a computer.

But what would be the result of taking the original 5 second sequence and playing back the tape at twice the speed? Same information but half the time to send. How would this affect bandwidth?

CHAPTER 3

WHAT IS VIDEO?

Video has many features based directly on the points discussed in the previous chapters. There are also new ones, particularly where colour is introduced, but these will not be dealt with until black and white video has been thoroughly investigated. The reason for this is because video first appeared as a black and white standard, which was later adapted to take colour. To understand colour, we must therefore fully appreciate the basic black and white system.

In our study of audio in telecommunications, we looked at a signal of continuously varying level or amplitude, with time. Audio is a serial signal that naturally converts to the electric signal of a two-wire circuit.

A picture signal is quite a different situation.

Sending pictures

The image in Figure 3.1 is constructed from pixels, or picture elements, the smallest detail that is discernible. In this case there are 100 of them, ten across and ten high. The image is virtually unrecognisable. The quality of the picture determines how many pixels are required, and clearly 10 × 10 is quite inadequate. Figure 3.2 requires many thousands to appear in the form shown here. This picture has been created by the photographer to achieve a specific response, but, as with all pictures, the final outcome depends on the observer. Our eyes never scan a scene consistently, they do not conform to any ordered sequence that could be reduced to a waveform as is done with audio. The consequence of this is that picture transmission has quite different criteria, particularly moving pictures.

We could send the picture as in Figure 3.3. The picture is broken into individual pixels, and each is connected to its own dedicated circuit that, in turn, connects to equivalent pixel of the picture display where the image will be reproduced. This is the parallel concept.

Figure 3.4 shows the analogy where the image is converted into serial form and passed into a single circuit. The pixels are sent one by one, and the action of image removal, or read-out, is a serial process. Compared to Figure 3.3,

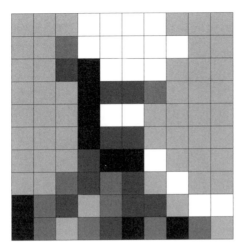

Figure 3.1   10 × 10 pixel array. Video uses a CCD (charge coupled device) image capture system. An electrical charge pattern is built up on a silicon pixel array that represents the light pattern of the focused scene. The charge is read off by a processor that converts it to a signal of serial form. A video camera may have up to half a million pixels.

Figure 3.2   A typical scene.

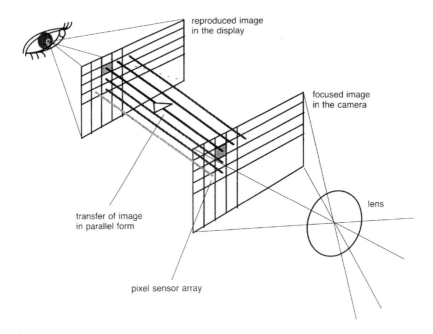

reproduced image
in the display

focused image
in the camera

lens

transfer of image
in parallel form

pixel sensor array

Figure 3.3   Parallel transfer of the image. All the picture elements are transmitted at the same time, in parallel. It is therefore expensive if the cable lengths are long. This principle of image capture and transfer is similar to the negative/positive process of film printing where the transfer is done with light. But, unlike film, video uses electrical connections.

this requires an order be applied: what the sensor does, the display must exactly follow. The signal must therefore carry the information about how the display is to reassemble.

Whether the parallel or serial method of transmission is used depends on, above all, how far the signal must travel.

In Chapter 2, where the correlation of time and information was looked at, it was seen how the two interrelate. Where pictures are involved, the transmission circuit becomes extremely significant. Were it possible, for instance, to take a whole day to send the image then the circuit demands are low. Raise the image rate and, over the same circuit, a lower quality reproduced picture would result. The two are interchangeable, and dependent on signal bandwidth. Where we require high quality pictures sent in real time, the circuit requirements rise very considerably. Video falls into this category.

The video system

The two video systems most widely used for domestic analogue transmission are the European PAL and the American/Japanese NTSC systems. Both are

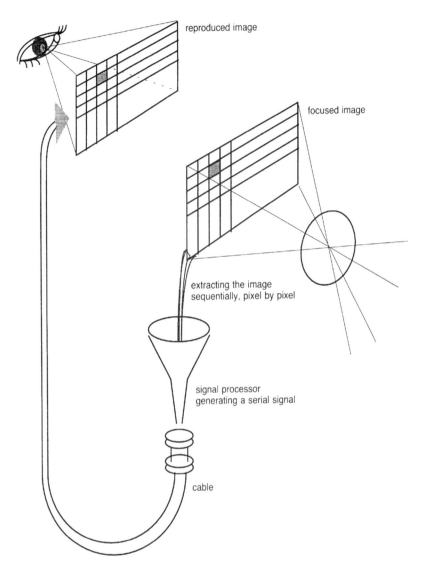

reproduced image

focused image

extracting the image
sequentially, pixel by pixel

signal processor
generating a serial signal

cable

Figure 3.4 Serial transfer of the image. The multiple connections of the parallel system are replaced by a single circuit. The focused image has to be dismantled into a pixel sequence that can be transmitted as a serial signal one pixel at a time.

similar in the technology they use, which determines that both have similar picture quality. For reasons of clarity, the PAL system will form the subject of the discussion, but where it becomes relevant, due to the inherent differences, the NTSC system will also be included. A third system, SECAM, is used for transmission in France, Russia, parts of Eastern Europe, and Africa.

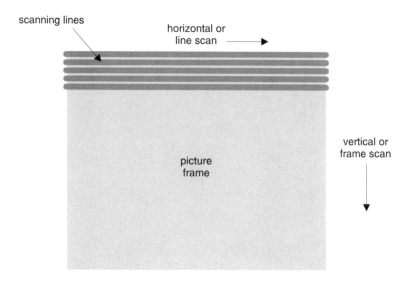

scanning lines

horizontal or
line scan

vertical or
frame scan

picture
frame

Figure 3.5 Scanning a picture frame. The image is scanned from top left to bottom right. 625 line video uses 25 pictures, or frames, per second.

Breaking the picture into horizontal lines and sending these one after the other was the technique chosen by early television engineers to transmit pictures down a cable. Figure 3.5 illustrates the concept. This produces a serial signal which may be sent over the two-wire circuit of video cable, or, as we often say, a single circuit. The PAL system uses 625 lines, the NTSC uses 525. These differences have far reaching implications, and why they came to be chosen is now embedded in history. Suffice to say that one may study these details elsewhere if one wishes.

The PAL standard is based on 25 separate pictures, or frames, every second, while NTSC runs at nearly 30. These are close to the 24 frames per second of cinematographic film. The first problem here is the visually annoying flicker rate. Film overcomes this by showing each frame twice, doubling the flicker rate from 24 to 48 times a second. The eye is much less sensitive to flicker at this rate. To overcome the problem with video a faster frame rate could have been chosen, but there is a penalty: that of bandwidth.

Let's look at the bandwidth requirements for a picture with 625 lines, 25 frames per second and a 4 by 3 aspect ratio. From Figure 3.6 the number of horizontal pixels can be determined as 833, and the time taken to trace each line works out to be 64 μs.

The finest scene detail which can be reproduced is where alternate pixels are exposed as in Figure 3.7. Here we see how bandwidth imposes a sine waveform on alternately exposed pixels, setting the upper bandwidth point. The finest picture detail translates into the maximum signal frequency thus

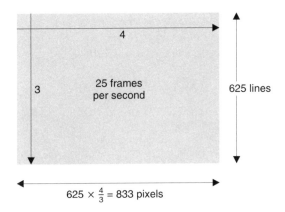

$$625 \times \tfrac{4}{3} = 833 \text{ pixels}$$

Figure 3.6 The 4 × 3 frame of 625 lines. The number of lines determines the vertical pixel count, one pixel per line. The same pixel density is required horizontally. At 25 frames per second and 625 lines per frame there are 15 625 lines per second. Therefore, the time taken for each line to cross the screen is:

$$\frac{1}{15\ 625} = 64 \times 10^{-6} \text{ seconds, or } 64 \ \mu s.$$

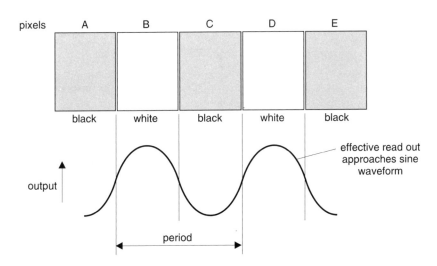

Figure 3.7 Alternate exposed pixels. Pixels A, C and E are unexposed, pixels B and D are fully exposed. These represent the maximum contrast of the scene and also its finest detail. When these are read off, the signal produced will have the maximum amplitude and resolution available from the sensor. The signal frequency produced from a sensor read-out having 833 horizontal pixels will therefore have a period *of twice the pixel size.*

obtained, and the circuit bandwidth is designed to have an upper frequency limit to accept this maximum. We can see the resulting waveform that corresponds to alternately exposed pixels will be 416 cycles for each line.

Therefore,

$$\frac{416 \text{ cycles per line}}{64 \times 10^{-6}\text{s}} = 6.5 \times 10^6 \text{ Hz or } 6.5 \text{ MHz}$$

The figure of 6.5 MHz is reduced to 5.5 MHz for the PAL transmission standard.

Increasing the frame rate from 25 per second to 50 to reduce flicker will require twice the bandwidth. We could halve the number of lines, use a frame rate of 50 per second and retain the same bandwidth. The flicker will be overcome but, of course, resolution, or picture detail, will be halved. Bandwidth is space, and space in the transmission spectrum is cost. Increasing bandwidth will also increase complexity and impose design restraints thereby causing additional cost penalties. It may even push the system beyond the technology available to build it.

A neat solution, using the manipulative ability of electronics, is to break each frame into two fields. By retaining the original frame rate of 25 per second for 625 lines we retain the same bandwidth for the same resolution, or very nearly so. Each frame is now made up of two fields, each with 312.5 lines.

The whole structure of the video picture is shown in Figure 3.8. Each line is traced out with a slight continuing movement (corresponding to the width of one line) down the picture. After every line there is a rapid flyback to commence the next. The fields are numbered 1 and 2 to identify them. Field 1 starts with a half line, field 2 ends with a half line. On completing a field, the scan returns to the top of the picture to start the next but, this time, displaced by half a line. The process repeats every two fields, making one frame.

When the bottom of the picture is reached, the scan returns to the top. All this action is conducted 'out of picture'. In fact, one can consider the picture as having a black frame where all the mechanics of picture construction go on unseen. With many displays the active scan size actually exceeds the physical size of the screen, thereby producing a cut off. Where the full scan is seen, electronic blanking, or reduction to black, ensures a clean straight edge all around the picture.

An implication of this is that not all lines are available to the actual picture. Twenty-five lines are taken up each field for the blanking period (20 lines in NTSC), totalling 50 out of the 625 for every frame. Although the number of active lines is now 575 (485 in NTSC), it is the full complement, including the blanked ones, which contribute to the total bandwidth requirement. An indicator of the waste of 'black screen'. And for wide-screen TV viewed in 'letterbox' format, where 50 per cent of the available picture may be lost to black, the bandwidth wastage is much higher.

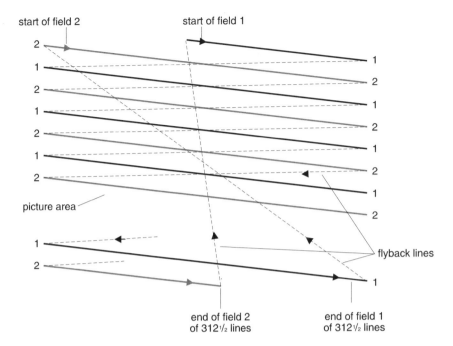

Figure 3.8 The interlaced frame. The picture display follows the same pattern as the image sensor with a scanned area larger than the actual picture. Each line commences outside the viewed area, a number of lines at the top of each frame are likewise unseen. Therefore, the number of 'active' lines is less than the total used.

The frame rate is the system's lowest frequency of 25 Hz. Note that the line rate frequency of 15.625 kHz is a multiple of 25 (that is, 25 × 625), making the resultant a complex waveform based on these two frequencies. Where scene detail gives rise to a signal with elements approaching the maximum of 5.5 MHz, as in Figure 3.7, then the waveform becomes very complex indeed. The bandwidth is now defined as 25 Hz to 5.5 MHz, which is quite near enough to state as simply 5.5 MHz.

Now we have seen how scanning the picture produces a serial signal that can be sent down a two-wire, or single circuit. At any instant in time, the signal has one value only, that of the brightness of a single pixel. We can say that the picture has been coded into an electric signal: the video signal.

Multiplexing video is, like audio, perfectly feasible, with similar benefits. For instance, sending six video signals over a 1000 MHz link takes up 39 MHz of space, plus a little more for good separation, say a total bandwidth of 40 MHz. That's only 4% of the spectrum at 1000 MHz. Sending at 2000 MHz (2 Gz) requires 2% of the spectrum. These examples are hypothetical but serve as an indicator to signal space requirements.

For those interested ...

Try calculating the bandwidth for a 50 frames per second video system. Use any number of lines. Decide a bandwidth and work back to find what sort of picture would be likely to fit into it.

The timebase

The picture display must accurately follow the original image scanning, whether this be from camera or other video source, if a successful reconstruction of the picture is to be achieved. Both source and display must start at exactly the same time, maintain step, and finish at the same time. This is called 'synchronism'. Should they get out of step the display will not know which part of the signal is which, will become confused and fail to reconstruct the picture.

Time is the fundamental parameter here. And time is relatively easy to measure electronically; our quartz watches are excellent examples of this. Consider a camera pointed at a scene, its electronic clock, or timebase, instructs the processor of the CCD sensor chip on which the image is focused, to start the sequence with line 1. However, before the camera actually commences scanning the picture, a marker is placed in the waveform that instructs the display to start its scan and await the arrival of the first line of the picture.

When the first line is complete another marker leaves the camera, telling the display to fly back and start the next line, and so on. At the bottom of the picture, at the end of field 1, a sequence of markers is generated by the camera saying the last line of that field has been sent and to return to the top of the picture and await the first line of field 2. We can see from this that there are two principal timing requirements: the line rate and the field rate. These are related, as we saw above.

It could be argued that it is not necessary to send timing information at each line. After all, modern clocks are very accurate and once started, the display could time itself by means of its own clock. However, it is synchronism that is the important element of video, not absolute time. Let's do a little calculation. In a one hour programme, there will be:

$$625 \times 25 \text{ frames} \times 60 \text{ seconds} \times 60 \text{ minutes} = 56\,250\,000 \text{ lines scanned}.$$

If the source and display clocks have an accuracy of 1 part in 100 000 ... typical of a quartz clock, then this could mean the clock times slipping by up to 562 lines during the one hour programme—an error that could amount to most of a frame out of sync. Even with a marker for every frame, such time keeping is still not good enough to ensure the displayed picture will not be distorted or fail entirely. Timing is therefore very important indeed and the scanning, or timebase, clock in a modern television receiver still needs constant timing updates to maintain the perfect synchronism required for good quality pictures.

What form do these timing markers take? In Figure 3.9 we see the waveform of a sequence of four lines, taken from the picture of a simple test signal. Between each line is a period of black, and it is here that the timing markers are placed. These are the line sync pulses and can be seen in Figure 3.10, which shows the waveform magnified to show one line in detail, and what these pulses look like. This is how picture and timing information are added together to complete the video waveform.

All these illustrations show an idealised representation of the waveforms. For instance, there are drawn instantaneous changes of level; there is an instant return from white to black at the end of the ramp, likewise, the sync pulses are shown with vertical edges. Although the discussion on bandwidth pointed out that this is not the case, in this diagrammatic style it is quite usual to show signals with vertical edges.

The scanning structure is, of course, invisible to the viewer; only the picture elements that are brighter than black will be seen. Therefore, to ensure that the correct values of black and white level are reproduced and no artefact of the process is seen, the standards for signal levels and timing are precise and must be adhered to.

The video waveform

The ramp waveform in Figure 3.10 is a signal that includes minimum and maximum amplitude in that it reaches from black to white level. These are the limits available to the picture maker and any excursion beyond these is prohibited and will normally be removed. That sync level is a further excursion need not concern those involved with the art of pictures. Unless, of course, they choose to know and read the whole of this book. The demarcation at black level need be no barrier to those who wish to understand.

The complete signal adds up to a maximum of 1 V, that is from sync level to white. But not all pictures possess a full range of tonal values and not every signal will utilise the system capacity. For example, not all pictures have white in them, nor do all pictures have black. The interesting case is where there is no picture at all—blank screen. The total picture is black.

Black is a common situation; there are often moments when a picture fades to black. However, this does not imply a lack of signal, far from it: all the timing requirements will still be present. The display must always be ready to show the fade-up from black to the next picture. Sync information must continue unbroken at all times.

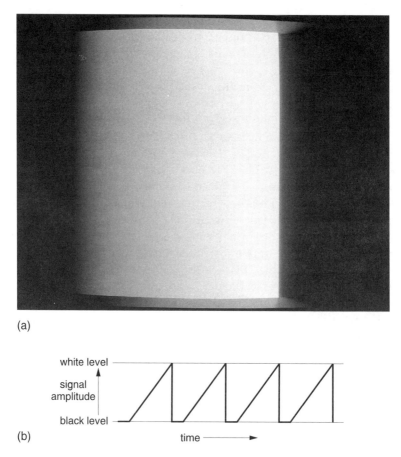

(a)

(b)

white level

signal
amplitude

black level

time

Figure 3.9   The ramp signal. The ramp signal appears on the picture monitor as in (a). It is a gradual shading from black to white, left to right. The name comes from its waveform shape. (b) shows four lines of waveform. Each line starts at black, rises to white, and then falls to black again. The black portion between successive lines is known as the line blanking period.

Figure 3.11 shows the standard video signal with the voltage values. Figure 3.12 is a picture waveform at black. Note the presence of sync pulses. This signal, often referred to as 'black and sync', is sometimes used for test purposes.

Black and white are the picture limits of the video system. The system will not allow any excursion below black. Although this may appear an unreal concept, 'blacker than black' is quite real in electronic terms for any value of signal may be represented by a specific voltage. So a limit is placed on picture information going below black, for, if not, there is the risk of confusion with sync pulses, and interference with the timing and synchronising process.

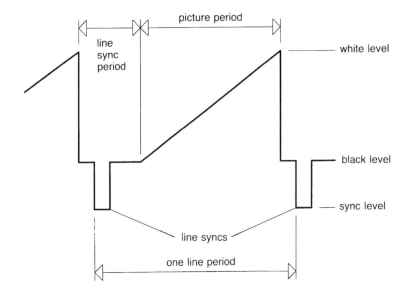

Figure 3.10   Ramp waveform and line sync pulses. Line sync pulses are inserted below black level in the blanked portion of the line and are therefore quite separate from the actual picture signal. They take the form of unseen voltage pulses outside the picture area and below black. Electronics and video make unreal concepts, such as blacker than black, perfectly possible when actual voltage values are added to the waveform.

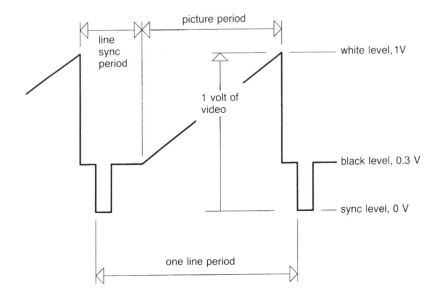

Figure 3.11   One volt of video
The ramp signal is shown running up from black at 0.3 V to white at 1.0 V. Sync level is the reference at 0 V, making black level 0.3 V and white 1.0 V. The picture, however, always occupies 70% of the waveform and the sync 30%. The term 'one volt of video' refers to the whole signal.

Figure 3.12   The picture at black. Even when there is no picture, timing information must still continue. The sync pulses remain intact regardless of picture content.

At black level, therefore, the picture is clipped right at the beginning in the camera. A similar limit is applied at white level, often known as 'peak white'.

The next stage is how and why we measure these values.

CHAPTER 4

MEASURING VIDEO

Why do we measure? Signals must fit into the system that carries them, if not, then the situation shown in Figure 4.1 will arise. All transmission systems, whatever the medium or method used, have maximum signal limits. Where signals exceed this maximum, distortion of the signal and the information it carries will occur. The form of distortion will depend on the system and how it has been misused, and the effect on the signal will depend on its resilience.

Figure 4.1 Insufficient headroom. The left-hand figure passes through the doorway easily. The one on the right is too tall. If a signal is too large the system will distort it and it is also likely that damage to other signals will occur where the system handles more than one at a time.

Signal level exceeding the standard limits is the most common distortion. Time is also subject to distortion. Signals take specific times to pass through systems and where these time delays, as they are called, are altered, we get signals arriving out of sync. Remember, that video is a time-based system. The implications of this will be gone into later.

Video is generated and sent as a voltage; we therefore require a voltmeter to measure it. Voltmeters are usually associated with steady-state conditions but video is not steady state. It is a constantly varying signal derived from a scanned picture. It also has the two distinct elements, picture and synchronising pulses, each needing their own specific measurement requirements. We must therefore have an instrument that allows us to 'see' the signal voltage as a waveform and to offer the means to observe and measure selectively.

We measure by placing a scale against that to be measured. A ruler measures in one dimension; video has two dimensions: level or amplitude, and time. The scale is called a grid, or graticule, as in Figure 4.2. Here, the two dimensions appear as X horizontally and Y vertically.

Figure 4.2 uses a typical measurement scale allowing measurement of all parts of the waveform to be done quickly. It is possible to alter the scale of measurement, not by changing rulers as it were, but by changing the amount we display. Figure 4.3 illustrates how two lines may be studied by doubling the observation time.

We must also state where our measurement references are. To do so we must establish the standard terms for various parts of the waveform, as in Figure 4.4.

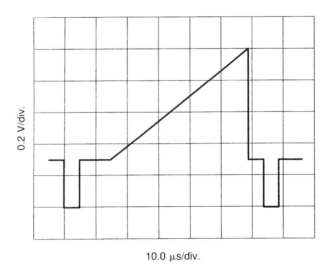

10.0 μs/div.

Figure 4.2 Placing a graticule over the waveform. The graticule is a measurement scale of both level and time. Measurement is done by shifting either the graticule or waveform until the section of interest is aligned against a graticule line. The scales here are: vertical, 0.2 V per division and horizontal, 10 μs per division. Note that the calibration is not absolute; we can choose where the scale is placed. As shown, the bottom of the line sync and the highest picture level are 5 divisions apart, which corresponds to 1.0 V. Horizontally, the time scale shows line sync as 5 μs wide and the distance between syncs as 64 μs. Note how the 1 cm squares are not sufficient for accurate measurement. Additional increments of 0.1 cm are usually added.

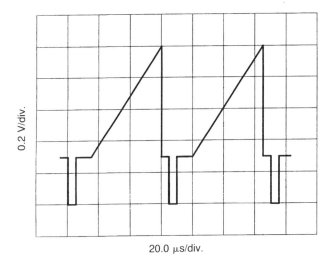

20.0 μs/div.

Figure 4.3 Doubling the observation time. The graticule remains the same as in Figure 4.2 but the time scale is now 20 μs per division, so permitting two lines to be seen.

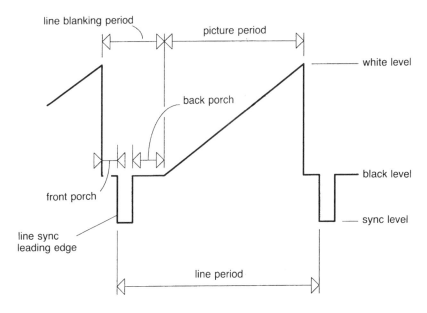

Figure 4.4 Terms in common usage. The line blanking period contains the line sync pulse, with **back and front porches**. The porches also represent video black level that separates the sync period from the picture. The line period may be measured between any two similar points, but it is usual to measure from leading edge to leading edge, of line sync.

Now for those who wonder about this term 'voltage' ...

Turn to Figure 4.2 and study the scale of measurement down the left-hand side; 0.2 volts per division. Measure the waveform voltage from sync to white level. Now imagine a battery being applied instead of the video waveform. How would it appear? A clue ... check the label on the battery.

Black level

Chapter 3 made reference to 'black'; that value in the picture where no light leaves the screen. We must now define this more carefully for it is crucial that the picture display knows exactly what this value really is.

We have seen how the video signal is made up of two distinct parts: the picture and the technical. The technical part is the sync information lying below black level. Black level not only provides separation between the two, but offers a picture black reference.

In Figure 4.2 the waveform shown has no absolute value, yet it is quite possible to measure the amplitude overall and its constituent parts. The maximum level, or peak white, is measured as 0.7 V above black. The absolute value of black is not stated and it is this that the picture display requires.

Any picture, to be reproduced accurately, must have its tonal values defined. It is insufficient to state these as relative values, i.e. that a face is brighter than the wall behind it. The level of brightness of the face must be converted into a signal value and, on arrival at the picture display, has then to be reproduced at the correct brightness. To do this we refer everything to black.

Now black may not exist in all pictures but it can be defined as a value in the video signal and a voltage value given to it. This reference value of black level is hidden in the sync period of the signal where the display can use it to construct all the tonal values in the picture.

As the signal passes through various circuits and systems, it may become subject to extraneous influences that result in the value of black level shifting. The value of black is very precise. Quite small variations can have very considerable impact on the picture reproduction. For instance, an inadvertent shift of picture black during signal transmission or processing by only a few per cent is far more critical than a change of overall level. The value of picture black must therefore be maintained throughout the transmission chain.

The video standard states that reference black will always be that of the back porch, the portion of picture blanking that precedes the picture.

Having established this, it becomes a simple procedure for the picture display to locate this point in the waveform, then to reference all picture tones to this, so ensuring that they are reproduced at their correct values. A picture may not contain black as defined in the waveform, but this does not alter the principle of sending a true video black level as a tonal reference.

In practice, black level can be allocated any convenient voltage. As long as peak white is at +0.7 V and sync level at −0.3 V with respect to the reference black level, the signal will still comply with the standard. Practical circuits, whether transmission or recording, may cause the absolute value of black level to change. Over practical distances of signal transmission, even a hundred metres of cable, interference from other apparatus may affect the signal, the most common form being that induced by adjacent power circuits. Picture displays, and other processing equipment must have, therefore, the means to recover the reference black from the video signal regardless of any distortion that may have taken place.

The process is known as 'DC restoration' and it is carried out at every line in the back porch. The term 'DC restore' means to restore the DC (direct current) component of the video signal. This action has become standard practice in signal processing and transmission.

The waveform monitor

The means to see a waveform has traditionally made use of the cathode ray tube. The principle is very similar to that used for picture displays but over the years there has been a divergence between the two designs. The waveform monitor, or WFM, has now become the established method of displaying waveforms. Figure 4.5 shows a basic CRT as used in waveform monitoring. Electrons, travelling at high velocity, are formed into a beam that, on passing under the influence of the voltage field between the deflection plates, becomes deflected. The signal must be raised to hundreds of volts for the beam to be fully deflected. The schematic diagram in Figure 4.6 shows in very simplified form how the signal drives the Y deflection plates in antiphase, that is, one plate swinging positive whilst the other swings negative.

Other forms of display are also in use, for instance the LCD (liquid crystal display) is becoming more common. Standard picture monitors may also double as WFMs by proprietary video adapters as will be seen later. All these variations use common parlance to describe the various functions. For the purpose of our discussion the CRT-based method will be used.

As we delve deeper into the complexity of video, so the rather simplified view of the waveform monitor of Figure 4.6 develops and adapts to the requirements of a practical system.

We have now put in place all the background to make measurement possible. There is a voltmeter in the form of a waveform monitor, WFM, able to measure signal level in voltage. We have ascertained the parameters of a

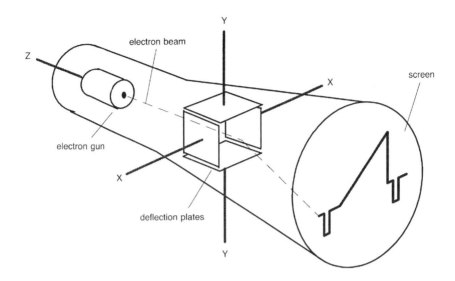

Figure 4.5   The cathode ray tube (CRT). The electron beam, travelling in a vacuum, strikes the phosphor coated screen causing light to be emitted. A voltage applied to the deflection plates results in electrostatic forces that deflect the beam. Plates YY carry the signal waveform, controlling the beam vertically, whilst XX carry the horizontal timing control. The Z connection to the electron gun allows the beam to be turned off during its return flyback.

standard signal and its references. Black level is established as the reference from which to measure picture levels. Overall amplitude is measured from the tip of sync pulses to the maximum permissible, which is white, sometimes known as 'peak white', and we have a time scale.

It is usual to state 'one volt of video' as the amplitude of a standard test signal. In the same way that actual pictures do not always possess black, they do not always possess white. One volt measures from sync level to white, whilst measuring from black level is generally carried out for picture-only information. Thus there is a distinction between measuring for test or engineering purposes and operational requirements.

Whichever is used, we need the means to position, or shift the waveform against the graticule. Figure 4.8 shows what this means and Figure 4.9 shows how it is done.

The complete WFM in Figure 4.10 is the basic layout and all the principal controls are shown. The timebase is switchable between different time values, the main ones are line and field, often abbreviated to H and V. For instance, 1H is one line, 2H is a display of two consecutive lines, but this does not quite explain what one is actually seeing. With the 1H mode, the timebase triggers the X deflection every line, resulting in a display of all lines superimposed.

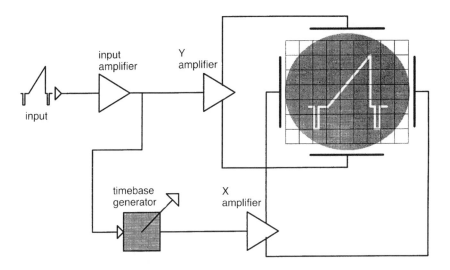

Figure 4.6 Principle of the waveform monitor. The input to the WFM is the video signal to be measured. The input amplifier passes the signal to the Y amplifier driving the Y plates controlling vertical beam deflection. The input amplifier also presents the signal to the timebase generator where the line syncs initiate a signal for the X plates that moves the beam across the screen at a steady rate. A timebase generator, running under the control of its internal clock synchronised to line sync pulses, produces the timing waveform for the X deflection. This action continually repeats with the horizontal deflection and flyback synchronised to the video signal. The timebase clock shown has a variable time rate (as indicated by the arrow), providing different time lengths over which the signal may be observed. In Figure 4.2 the display is shown at line rate whilst Figure 4.3 is twice line rate as determined by the clock rate.

Figure 4.11 shows how this appears and for comparison, a display of just one line. Note, the latter may appear less bright for it only has one line's worth of energy every $\frac{1}{50}$th of a second, whereas the former has a whole field of $312\frac{1}{2}$ lines over the same period.

Exactly the same applies when considering the field display. Selecting V shows one field, 2V is of both the fields making up one frame. A 2V display is as shown in Figure 4.12.

Magnification of the display is very similar to using an optical magnifying glass. The shift controls move the expanded waveform until the desired part is placed in the graticule. Magnification rates of 5 to 25 times are common. As only a portion of the waveform now occupies the screen the image is theoretically less bright, a situation rectified by increasing the display brightness.

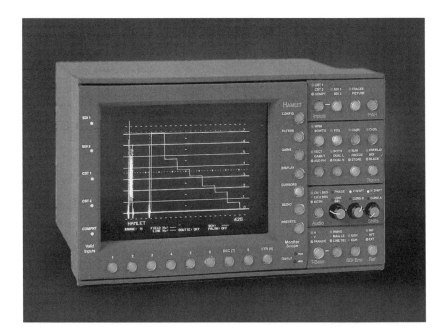

Figure 4.7   Universal signal measurement. The Hamlet Monitor Scope 601 combines picture monitor, WFM, vector display, and audio, into a single unit with an LCD colour screen. The low power requirements make possible comprehensive portable measurement of both analogue and digital video.

Brightness of the display is an operational control made necessary by the variation of ambient lighting conditions encountered in practice. To compensate for brightness variation brought about by changing the time-scale and magnification, an automatic system is usually incorporated into the instrument. It is only possible to increase brightness to that allowed by the screen. Attempting to go beyond this point is liable to distort and make the display less sharp.

Timing and system sync

We have ascertained that video is a time-based system. The information about picture tonal values is sent as a voltage broken down into a sequence of lines and fields. Information about which part of the picture is which is therefore part of a timed sequence. The video standard sets out the timing values of the signal so that any standard picture display will function with picture generating apparatus designed to the same standard.

Timing standards must be as rigorously adhered to as amplitude values. For example, two cameras linked to a studio video mixer or switcher, must

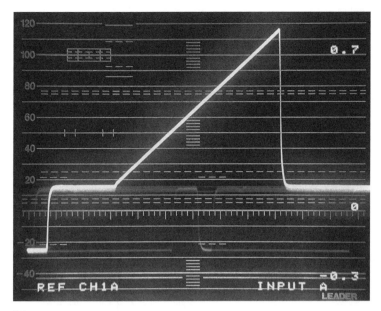

(a)

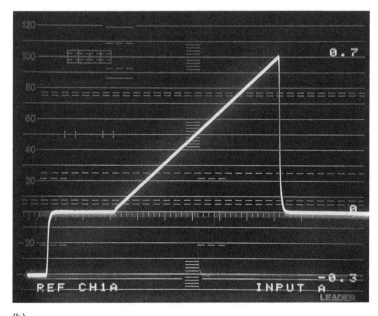

(b)

Figure 4.8   Measuring the video signal. These pictures show the relative shift of waveform against graticule. (a) is positioned too high; (b) has black level positioned correctly, with white at 0.7 V and sync at –3 V, as indicated by the read-out. The graticule has 10% steps from black at 0% to white at 100%. The time scale is shown along black level in main divisions of 5 μs subdivided into 1 μs. Other markings have specific purposes.

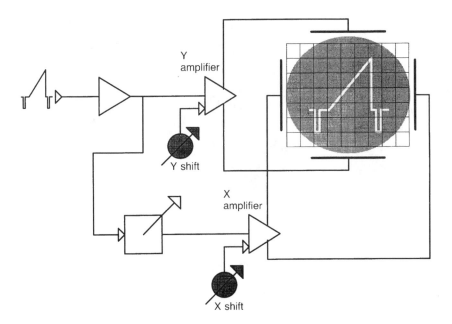

Figure 4.9   Positioning the signal against the graticule. Shift controls
are additive inputs to the deflection amplifiers that allow variable DC (positive
or negative) to be added to both the signal and timebase deflection drives.
They make the display position adjustable against the graticule.

produce signals in synchronism. If not, then, as the switcher cuts or mixes
the two pictures, confusing synchronising information will be sent out.

We have already seen the importance attached to the signal's sync pulses.
They carry the timing information, which tells picture displays in studio and
the home when pictures start and end. Should our two cameras produce
pictures that are not synchronous, conflict will arise as to which camera the
display is to follow.

There are therefore, two criterion, timing accuracy of the signal, the period
(or time length) of lines and fields, and timing synchronism between picture
sources. The WFM deals with both of these but in different ways. Line and
field period is measured against the time period generated by the WFM's
timebase. When time synchronism is to be measured we must choose one of
the cameras to be master and compare the timing position of the other to it.

It is the latter situation that provides the WFM with a large part of its
duties. Signal time values are standard and as such are designed into the
picture generating equipment, whatever that may be. Such parameters are
unlikely to vary unless a fault condition arises.

On the other hand, synchronism is a system feature, with operational
requirements. Systems are designed for specific work, e.g. the design of our
two-camera studio must ensure that both cameras are synchronous at the

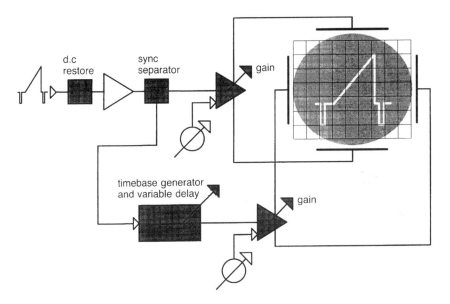

Figure 4.10 The complete waveform monitor. The dc restore circuit at the signal input gives black level a precise value and places black at the same point on the graticule regardless of how the picture values change. The sync separator is a sophisticated circuit that provides precise timing from the sync pulses for the timebase generator. The timebase generator offers variable delay of the Y deflection so that any particular line may be displayed. The deflection amplifiers have a variable gain (variable control of amplitude), to provide the detailed study of signal level.

switching point. Remember, signals travel at a finite rate, although this approaches the speed of light, it is significant when compared to line rate. Cable lengths now become important. Should one camera be at the other side of the studio on a long length of cable, its signal will be later than one placed closer on a shorter length.

The problem is resolved by using the WFM to compare the cameras to its own timebase, or camera to camera. Figure 4.13. This, however, does not tell the whole story. If the WFM is selected to each switcher source in turn, each signal will be placed on exactly the same part of the display; the WFM sync separator and timebase would see to that. Although signal level differences will be seen, timing differences will not. Figure 4.14 illustrates how this is overcome.

So how close must timing be? A basic system should be timed to an accuracy of 0.5 μs or better. Figure 4.15 shows typical timing measurement. This rather simplified view leaves much still untold, and we shall see in subsequent chapters how the subject develops. With the introduction of colour a whole new dimension to video opens up.

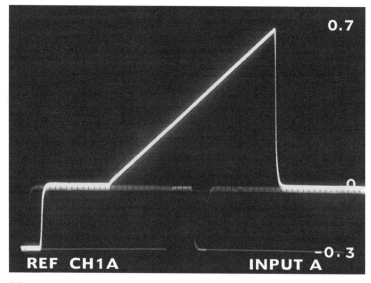

(a)

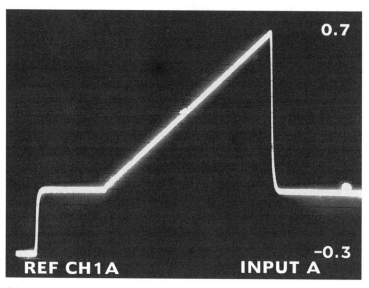

(b)

Figure 4.11   Line rate and single line displays. All lines are shown over-laid in (a); this is the 1H display. Note there is a spurious signal at black and sync levels. These are the black lines and field sync pulses of the field sync period. In (b), only one active picture line is shown. In both pictures, the graticule light is turned off to show the effect more clearly.

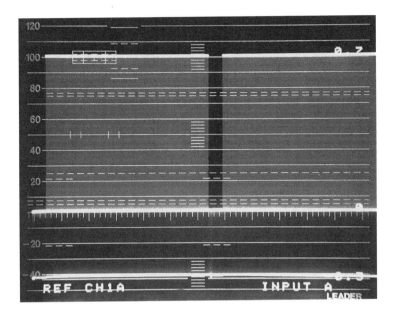

Figure 4.12 Field rate display. The two-field (2V) waveform consists of all lines shown sequentially but are so close together that they loose individual identity. The black lines of the field sync period are clearly shown. The line sync appears as a continuous line but it is possible to see the brightening of the field sync pulse. The time scale is $\frac{1}{25}$ s or 40 ms.

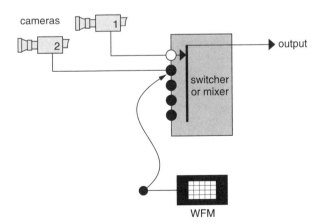

Figure 4.13 A simplified studio system. The switcher, or mixer, is the heart of the system. Camera 1 is shown selected to the output. The WFM is checking camera 2.

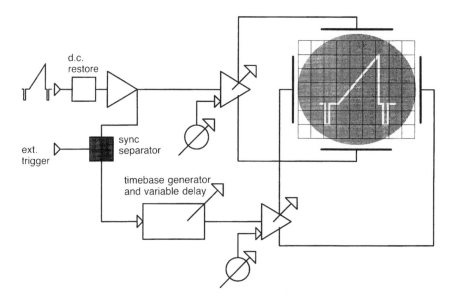

Figure 4.14 Synchronising the WFM. Rearranging the WFM sync separator with its own dedicated input makes the WFM able to display timing differences. Connecting one of the cameras to 'Ext Trigger' makes the WFM 'lock' to one sync only. Other cameras and sources can now be displayed against this master by connecting these in turn to the main WFM input.

'Scopes versus WFMs

At this point it is worthwhile looking at how the WFM differs from the conventional waveform display of the oscilloscope. The 'oscilloscope', often shortened to 'scope or CRO (cathode ray oscilloscope), differs very little in principle from its progeny the WFM. Both show voltage vertically and time horizontally. Indeed, the 'scope may often be seen used in place of a WFM but it is the operational differences that distinguish the two.

With a more specialist instrument, dedicated controls and circuitry become standard. Because the WFM is specifically designed for video, it uses video sync separation to achieve reliable triggering at line and field rates. There is the ability to delay the display for a specified time to study any part of the scanning sequence. For example, the field trigger starts a counter that counts the lines down to the point to be observed, then releases the display for that line. There are features which specifically apply to PAL and NTSC composite video, such as subcarrier filters and aspects of SC-H phase which is explained in more detail in the Appendix.

The WFM will have the option to select DC restoration enabling black level always to be placed at the same point on the graticule.

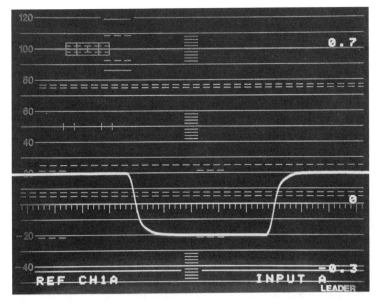

(a)

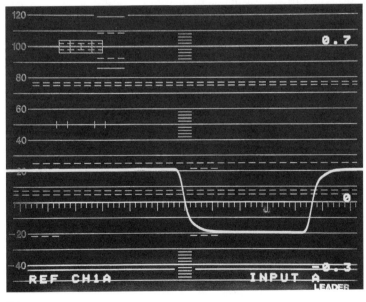

(b)

Figure 4.15 Timing the signal. These are the line syncs of two cameras (see Figure 4.13) magnified horizontally five times. (a) shows the waveform aligned horizontally to bring the sync leading edge to the centre and placed against a convenient time-scale point. (Note how the vertical shift has been adjusted upwards.) When the other camera is selected as in (b), its timing is seen to be late by 2 μs. Although there is no picture information on the waveforms, the signals are 'black and sync', the test may be carried out just as easily in the presence of pictures.

The 'scope is designed to be a versatile measurement and fault finding tool. Its input circuitry is designed for minimum effect on the systems and circuitry and the wide range of time and voltage scales available make it versatile. It is designed to accommodate a variety of waveforms, all shapes and amplitudes, audio, power and even DC. Many 'scopes do offer additional video facilities but video is so complex with important parts of the waveform difficult to study with conventional displays, that the WFM has become a standard part of the video system.

New display methods

Liquid crystal displays (LCDs) are finding their way into all forms of presentation. The principle is quite different to the cathode ray tube. Instead of a single spot scanning the screen, the LCD is based on a pixel matrix (Figure 4.16).

The LCD has inherent benefits over the CRT, and two of these stand head and shoulders above the rest. Size and shape, and power consumption. The LCD is a flat screen with a small 'footprint', and is ideal for cramped mobile installations. It also lends itself well to battery operation. Another

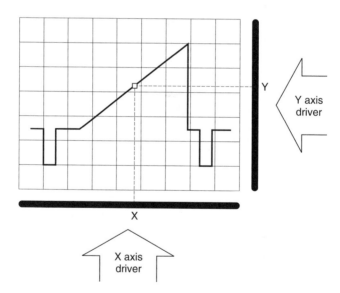

Figure 4.16   The LCD display. The LCD display utilises digital techniques. The signal is converted to digital form and processed into X, Y and Z co-ordinates. X and Y are as before, Z is brightness modulation. Each pixel has an address based on the X and Y co-ordinates, the pixel described by x and y will also be given a brightness value. Comprehensive digital processing, with colour screen, also makes picture monitoring a very useful option. A typical LCD WFM is shown in Figure 4.7.

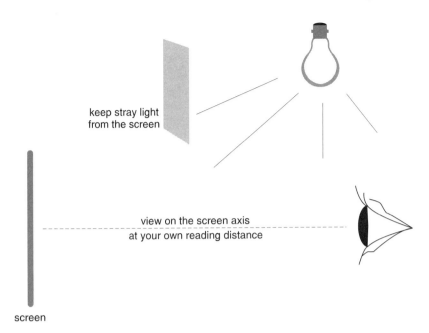

keep stray light
from the screen

view on the screen axis
at your own reading distance

screen

Figure 4.17   Good viewing conditions. Ideal conditions are often not possible. But the better they are and the more comfortable you are, the less chance there is of making an error. Viewing on the screen axis avoids parallax error arising where the graticule is spaced away from the display.

consideration is that the LCD is gaining popularity and so prices can be expected to fall as production volumes rise. On the other hand, the CRT is power hungry and a less convenient shape. However, it has, over the years benefited from extensive development until it is now so well refined that it cannot be lightly dismissed. For many installations, the CRT-based instrument still offers an ideal solution.

Using the WFM

Measuring the signal requires the same care as measuring anything else: the correct conditions and a steady eye. This means being in a comfortable position, with the WFM also comfortably placed. CRT-based WFMs produce light and are therefore quite susceptible to ambient light falling on the screen. LCDs have a backlight and the same conditions therefore apply.

Actual situations will invariably use picture monitoring as part of the overall test and measurement environment; viewing pictures will itself dictate control of ambient light. Figure 4.17 sets out the main issues.

CHAPTER 5

ADDING COLOUR

It is an established principle that any colour may be described in terms of red, green and blue (RGB). These are the colour primaries of additive colour; the distinction between adding coloured lights together and reflecting white light from coloured dyes is very important. Additive colour is that produced by the screen of a TV or monitor, where red, green and blue in equal amounts add to make white light (see Figure 5.1).

We must also establish a few other principles before a full understanding of colour can be gained, starting with the picture. Where the picture display screen produces no light, the result is black (assuming ideal viewing conditions with no reflected ambient light). Where the screen produces the maximum possible of each colour, the output is white. Between these two limits is an infinite number of levels. At intermediate, but equal levels of red, green and blue, the colours add to make grey.

In practice, the black of one picture display may differ from that of another, depending on its design. The same applies to the maximum light output available. A consequence of this is that actual values of black and white are not absolute, they will vary from screen to screen. Standards must therefore be established before a working system is possible.

Colour components

The choice of colours to use—which of red or green or blue—was dictated by the availability of phosphors for the CRTs used in early colour television. That standard still applies but there has been a steady improvement in this field over the years. The one principle that does remain is that equal values of RGB produce grey and this has become established in the video standard. Whatever the picture source or processing applied, this standard always applies.

The values in Figure 5.2 may be set down as voltage levels, i.e. 0 V to 0.7 V, and these values would apply to inputs as well as outputs where the signals are sent over standard circuits.

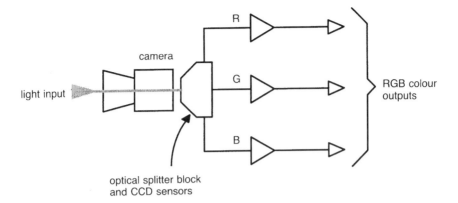

Figure 5.1   The three-colour video camera. The light is split into red, green and blue by a dichroic optical block and converted by CCDs into RGB signals. The three-colour CCD camera is universal in the television industry.

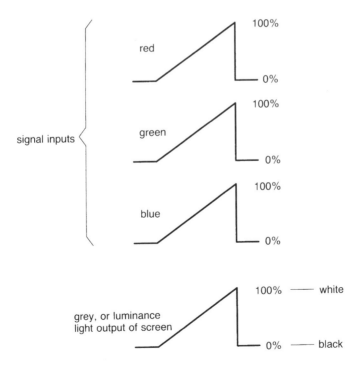

Figure 5.2   Additive colour. The ramp test signal is sent to the three colour channels of a picture display and produces continuous variation of grey tone.

The video standard states that when all the colour signals have the same level the result is grey. Therefore:

when R = B = G = 0 the result is black

when R = B = G = 100% the result is white

when xR + xB + xG = xY where xY is the equivalent luminance,

   or grey, value.

Where the scene has only one colour present, say, red, neither green nor blue will be present. Other colours are a mixture of red, green and blue in various amounts. There are also the colour opposites to red, green and blue, which are cyan, magenta and yellow. These are the complimentary colours, and result when one of the primaries is not present:

R + B = Magenta. (Green is not present.)

R + G = Yellow. (Blue is not present.)

B + G = Cyan. (Red is not present.)

Colour pictures may be sent as RGB signals, but this is not a particularly efficient way to do so. RGB requires three identical circuits, and the use of three circuits incurs three times the cost. All three circuits must be identical in every respect with all signals experiencing the same processing. If either of these is not adhered to, the principle of equal values will be violated and colour distortion will occur.

There are, however, features in the way we see which enable some parameters to be modified and simplifications made. Our ability to see fine detail in colour is less than in black and white; colour can, therefore, have a lower specification with regard to how much detail information is sent. Lower resolution colour signals directly translate into a bandwidth saving. Our vision is more sensitive to differences of hue than of saturation and we are more aware of colour changes than we are of colour intensity. Another factor is that we are most sensitive to green, our eye's acuity peaks in the green part of the spectrum. Of all three colours, green most closely resembles the luminance signal.

Because of the way we perceive colour, benefits can be gained in the design of the system and the way pictures are transmitted.

As the black and white signal is so important in its own right, it is advantageous to separate it from the colour signal. Having done so, there is little point in sending the full RGB colours since each contains an element of luminance. Taking these factors together, the answer is to send luminance, plus the red and blue colour *difference* signals, that is the red and blue colours signals *minus* luminance. Green, because of its similarity to luminance, need not be sent for we only need two colour difference signals with luminance to reconstruct the complete colour picture.

We now come up against another of video's unrealisable conditions. Earlier, we met the concept of 'blacker than black' when discussing the video waveform. Now it is colour without brightness (we should be strict and use the term 'luminance'). These are mathematical postulations, and have no tangible form. There will be more, and the reader must accept them for what they are: manipulations by electronics.

The Y signal has the advantage in that it is the complete black and white signal and a usable picture is still available should the colour signals get lost, or if a black and white picture is all that is required. The colour signals may be specified for colour resolution only, so trading off unnecessary signal capacity. This then is the basis of component video and is shown as:

Y   luminance, all colours adding to make the black and white signal

R – Y   red minus luminance

B – Y   blue minus luminance

Green is recovered with a little mathematics worked out by the electronics in the picture display.

The requirement for all three signals to be maintained at the correct levels still applies. Should they vary then colour errors, both in hue and saturation, will arise.

Colour bars

The ramp test signal is a black and white signal and has limitations when applied to colour operation. Figure 5.2 shows how the three RGB channels carrying identical ramp signals achieve a black and white ramp output.

The representation of colour values is best seen with the standard colour test signal, colour bars. This waveform is also useful to us in learning more about the colour system. Figure 5.3 illustrates, with colour bars, the relationship between the colour signals and luminance. How the colour difference signals are achieved is evident from the graphical representation. Again, a little maths is involved, and note . . . all signals are normalised to 100%, and equivalent to a maximum signal excursion of 0.7 V.

Subtracting Y from either of the colour signals will produce both a negative and positive going resultant; a symmetrical signal. The blue component is the greater with nearly 90% above and below the axis, a total swing of almost 180%. The red has a total swing of 140%. Compare these to the normalised maximums of 100% for the RGB and Y signals and it will be evident they exceed the 1 V standard. Although it may, at this point, be argued that we are

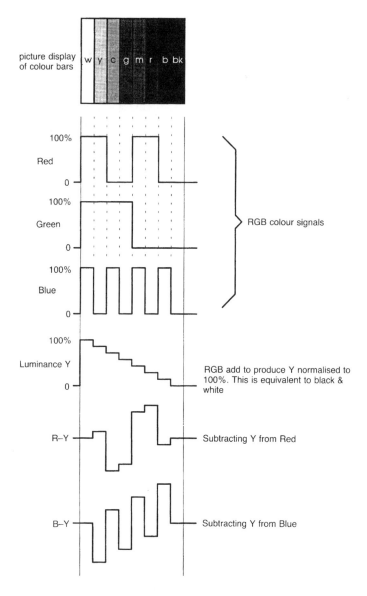

Figure 5.3 Colour bars and colour difference. Colour bars represent the limits of colour and black and white signals. The three components, RGB, each have a luminance element. Subtracting Y from RGB produces colour-only signals. Note how the R – Y and B – Y signals are much higher in amplitude than the individual RGB and Y signals; this results from subtracting the luminance value from a colour of lower value, producing a negative signal swing where the complimentary colours occur.

considering only approximations, these are quite close enough to illustrate the discussion.

The high amplitude values of the colour difference components shown in Figure 5.3 are wasteful; the colour information in actual pictures is really quite small and does not justify this amount of signal space. A more equable solution is therefore to reduce the amplitudes of R − Y and B − Y to more realistic values. This would of course upset the principle of additive colour, but by restoring the original values, using the reverse calculation, at the picture display, the answer will turn out the same. The colour difference signals are therefore weighted to bring their amplitudes into line with standard values.

In doing this, we make yet another standard which must be agreed by system designers at either end of a circuit. There is also an inherent practical problem. Reducing the value of a signal before sending means it must be amplified on its arrival. This will compromise the performance where noise is concerned because noise will be amplified as well as signal but, as we have already said, we can accept some kinds of colour degradation, and colour noise is one of these. Blue, the least critical in this regard, has maximum weighting; it was the larger of the two in the first instant and its weighted value is half that of the original.

The weighted values of the component signals, as applied to colour bars, are listed in Table 5.1.

The weighted red component has a higher value allocated to it than blue, reflecting the greater importance attached to red. Note also how the colour compliments have equal but opposite values to their respective primaries, e.g. green/magenta.

The colour difference signals go below zero to swing negative, producing the subtractive colour elements (for instance, minus blue is yellow). In consequence, it may be thought that such signals contravene the rule about the signal going below black level. A distinction has therefore to be drawn between standards for luminance and colour difference signals. As a consequence, only the luminance signal carries synchronising information, there

Table 5.1 Weighted values of colour bars

	R − Y (%)	B − Y (%)
Yellow	10	−44
Cyan	−62	15
Green	−52	−29
Magenta	52	29
Red	62	−15
Blue	−10	44

is neither need nor benefit in more than one set of sync pulses going to the same destination.

The figures in Table 5.1 represent the maximum permitted, here shown as percentage. Because these values normalise to 100% they are known as 100% colour bars.

Transmitting pictures and composite video

Now is a suitable time to take an overview of the video system. We have come a long way from the two-wire single circuit and already we are grappling with the esoterics of colour television. This, of course, belies the true situation, the huge amount that goes on behind the waveforms and pictures. Nor does it do justice to the work of those who created colour television.

Such was the success of the system devised for colour TV that its influence has been far reaching, and still is. Above all was the demand that colour should make no greater demand on the transmission systems than did black and white. A tall order indeed, considering colour requires not one, but three circuits. However, where pictures have to be sent any great distance, the use of three circuits is a serious disadvantage. For national TV transmission it is prohibitive. Essentially, the original black and white video waveform described in the previous chapters is adapted to accept the addition of colour. The bandwidth requirements remain similar, and allow similarly specified circuits to be used. In practice, there is a marginal upgrade in equipment specification. But we have a three-colour signal in one video cable. This is composite video.

The first step toward this is to reduce the three colour signals from RGB to luminance, Y, the original black and white signal, and the two colour-difference signals, $R - Y$, $B - Y$. The latter are combined into a high-frequency sine wave carrier by a process called modulation, to form the chrominance signal, often written as simply 'C' (the terms 'colour subcarrier', 'subcarrier', 'CSC', or 'SC' may also be found but are not strictly correct for these relate to the *un*-modulated carrier).

Finally, Y and C are added together to form the composite signal. The result: one signal, and one cable.

The Appendix explains colour encoding and decoding, but the main principles may be summarised here:

1 The composite signal consists of two parts; luminance, Y, and chrominance, C.
2 The Y element is the basic black and white signal.
3 C is the combined colour difference signals encoded into a subcarrier, CSC.
4 Colour saturation is carried by the amplitude of subcarrier. Where colour is zero, so the subcarrier will be zero.

5 Hue is carried by the phase of the subcarrier relative to a colour reference marker.

Hue changes, to which the eye is so sensitive, are carried by the phase angle of the subcarrier and it is relatively easy to build in safeguards to protect this from becoming changed. The amplitude of the subcarrier is, however, more vulnerable but as this determines saturation, a less critical parameter, the effect on the viewer is minimised.

On arrival at the receiver, after what may have been a long and difficult journey, the signal could have suffered degradation and it is quite likely that the original waveform is less than perfect. The all-important information it carries must, however, still be recoverable. To do this, reliable decoding of the chrominance and unravelling the complexity of phase and amplitude variation, must be achieved. A practical picture contains all values of colour hue and saturation in varying degrees. To ensure the decoding is carried out accurately after the addition of transmission noise and disturbance, an accurate colour reference is sent as part of the composite signal.

The colour burst

To recover the colour information the TV receiver, or picture display, 'looks' for subcarrier. In areas of high colour it is easily found but it will be elusive in areas near grey, and none at all in where only true grey exists. Chrominance is, by its very nature, a complex waveform and there is only one way to extract the colour information.

By sending a colour reference, we provide the means for the receiver to regenerate its own subcarrier of identical frequency and phase to that in the signal. A simple quartz oscillator is too inaccurate. Back in Chapter 3, we saw the requirements of video timing and how the accuracy of quartz clocks falls short of video timing requirements. By adding a short burst of subcarrier, called the colour burst, to each line, a permanent clock reference is sent along with the signal. The decoder is now able to look for picture subcarrier simply because 'it knows where to do so' (see Figure 5.4).

Figure 5.5 shows the various components that make up colour bars in composite video. As colour bars represent the maximum values permitted it has established itself as the universal test signal. Current practice now states that 100% colour bars exceed the practical requirements of normal pictures, and a less saturated version based on 75% colour saturation values has come into common usage (see Figure 5.6).

Colour and vectors

The separation of colour and luminance has become established in many areas of video operation. A number of variations of component

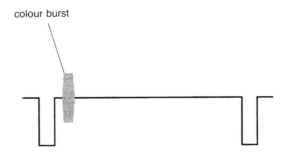

colour burst

Figure 5.4 Line waveform with colour burst. Colour burst is 10 cycles of subcarrier preceding the picture on each line, it is also present during most of the field period. It has a very precise and accurately maintained phase relationship to the rest of the signal. The colour burst amplitude is 0.3 volts peak-to-peak (0.3 Vpp). The sync detection circuits in receivers, etc. are designed to ignore the negative excursion of subcarrier below black level. The waveform shown has no picture information and is therefore often called 'colour black', or 'black and burst' or 'sync and burst'. At the point of encoding, the colour burst must be accurately generated and maintained for it is this small part of the composite signal that provides both phase and amplitude information essential to the correct reproduction of colour. Colour burst serves to synchronise the decoder oscillator so that a perfect replica of the original subcarrier is accurately regenerated, perfectly stable in phase and amplitude.

$(Y, R - Y, B - Y)$ video exist, adapted to different requirements and situations. The use of vector analysis has, in the main, been associated with composite video, but there is no reason why the principle should not be considered as an aid to understanding more about colour.

Colour information carried by the phase and amplitude of subcarrier may be translated into a vector, that is, its phase and amplitude corresponds to the vector co-ordinates. In Figure 5.7, we can imagine, as observers, the subcarrier sine wave streaming by, its voltage rising and falling with each passing cycle at frequency rate. We can also illustrate the action as a rotating vector that follows the voltage swing, not along a continuous axis, but about a fixed point. Take the argument one step further, place ourselves alongside the wave and travel with it at exactly the same speed. Now the wave appears stationary. If we could do the same with the vector, it too would be stationary. This is what the decoder does: 'freezes' the wave. It's rather like the stage coach wheels in a western; when they run at the same speed as the camera shutter, the spokes appear still, when the coach slows down they slip back, and vice versa. That's the relative phase shifting about, an effect we call strobing, but in electronics it's known as synchronous detection.

By having its own regenerated CSC locked to the incoming colour burst, the picture display is able to synchronise its observation of the signal to measure against this reference, the phase and amplitude of chrominance

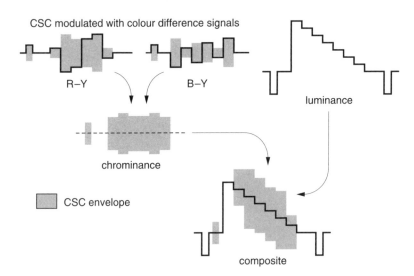

Figure 5.5 Colour bars in composite signal form. The colour difference signals are modulated onto the CSC, their original forms are overlaid for comparison. Note that where there is no colour, i.e. black and white bars, there is no subcarrier. The colour burst is created with the colour difference signals and becomes part of the modulated envelope. The colour difference signals are added together to make the completed chrominance signal. Finally, chrominance and luminance are combined to form the composite signal.

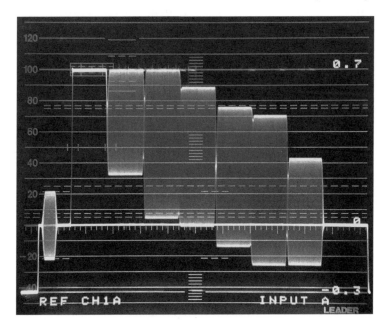

Figure 5.6 WFM display of colour bars. 75% colour bars. The WFM is unable to display any information about colour apart from saturation which shows as the amplitude of chrominance.

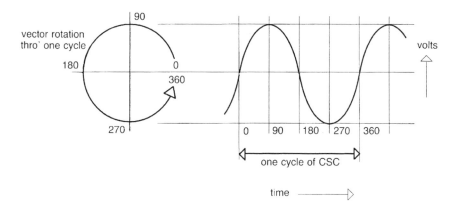

Figure 5.7   Vector rotation of a sine wave. The vector constantly rotates to follow the sine wave's instantaneous voltage; as it passes through zero volts, the vector is at either 0°, 180° or 360°. One complete rotation is 360°. By observing the vector at exactly the same point in the cycle, the vector will appear stationary. The length of the vector represents the sine wave amplitude at a specified point in time.

information. Now we see the colour as stationary points in a circular display, and therefore hue and saturation are very quickly and easily examined.

Figure 5.8 uses the colour values of colour bars to show how a vector representation of colour is built up. As the colour varies along the line so the vector values change accordingly. Should the CSC shift phase through one complete cycle, that is 360°, it will return to its starting point. In doing so the vector will rotate through the whole colour spectrum. There are (theoretically, at least) an infinite number of possible colours in one 360° sweep, all having a specific vector value.

With the colour spectrum held in this way, the ability of the receiver to measure small phase angles is crucial to accurate colour reproduction. The colour burst gives a reference of phase, every line against which the CSC phase variations on that line are compared, and from which the colour difference components are reconstructed. To get some idea of the accuracy required, let us work out how long 360° of CSC represents.

The subcarrier frequency of PAL is 4.43361875 MHz, therefore, the length of one cycle is:

$$\frac{1}{4.43361875\text{ MHz}} = 0.225549388\ \mu s$$

... and for NTSC:

$$\frac{1}{3.579545\text{ MHz}} = 0.2793725\ \mu s$$

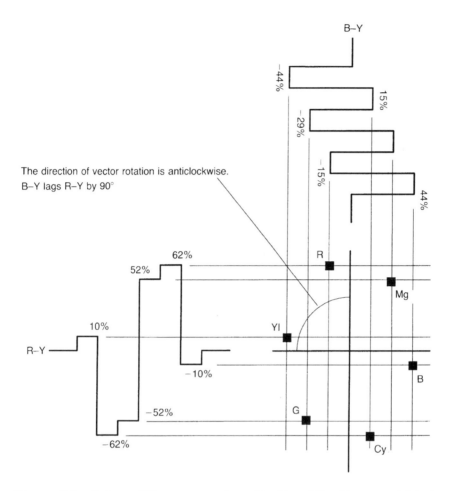

Figure 5.8 Colour difference vectors. R – Y and B – Y are modulated onto the subcarrier, with B – Y delayed by 90°. Therefore, as shown here, R – Y amplitude is shown *vertically* and R – Y amplitude is shown *horizontally*. The signal colour values extend and meet at the vector co-ordinates that specify hue and saturation by vector angle and length. Angle is measured from the horizontal axis starting at '3 o'clock'. The vector for magenta on this diagram could therefore be specified as:

$$\sqrt{(52^2 + 29^2)} = 60\% \text{ at, } \tan^{-1}\frac{52}{29} = 61°$$

Considering that the whole colour spectrum is held within these time periods, only a very small variation of timing will introduce a noticeable colour change. In fact, variations of greater than about 0.005 µs are likely to be observed. Earlier, we saw how the video system relied on timing to synchronise picture displays to picture generators. A timing accuracy figure for black and white television of about 0.5 μs was considered good enough. The figure of 0.005 μs is one hundred times more accurate and requires a very different approach.

If the standard requires an accuracy of 5°, then, 360/5 = 72, is the available hue resolution.

Rationalising the two standards for convenience and letting one cycle of subcarrier be 0.25 μs, we can see that getting 72 colours squeezed into this time-scale means working to within 3 or 4 nanoseconds.

With this timing specification required for colour phase in composite video, measurement is beyond the conventional WFM. But by separating the chrominance out and observing that alone, the problem becomes much more easily dealt with. Now colour can be most easily observed by using the values derived from the colour vector values of phase and amplitude.

Measuring timing values for synchronism now splits into luminance, which we have already discussed in Chapter 4, and chrominance.

NTSC and PAL

Further differences now begin to emerge between the NTSC system and its European derivative, PAL.

The eye offers other features that the composite signal is able to utilise in the interests of fine tuning the system. We are able to resolve fine colour detail better in the red/orange part of the spectrum than in the blue/cyan. Bandwidths of the colour signals can therefore be adjusted to take advantage of this but to do so effectively, their axes should be realigned.

The NTSC system advances the modulation axes by 33° from the original R − Y and B − Y axes to those approximating to orange/red and blue/cyan. These new axes are called I and Q respectively, the Q axis carrying blue/cyan, having less bandwidth than the orange/red I axis. Trading bandwidth where it is not needed in this way makes it available elsewhere in the signal. PAL does not make use of this feature and does not use I and Q modulation axes. Instead PAL reduces bandwidth of both R − Y and B − Y, calling them V and U respectively.

Although NTSC and PAL are technically incompatible, their basic principles are similar.

Phase errors

The main difference between PAL and NTSC is the additional protection PAL offers against the effects of phase variation and the colour distortion this brings. Let us now look at how this affects the picture.

Because hue is described by the phase or vector angle, and a 5° shift is considered the maximum permissible error, the whole system becomes extremely sensitive to timing. In standard coaxial video cable the signal travels at about two-thirds the velocity of light and over a typical studio length, say 50 m, the signal will take about 250 ns (0.250 μs), to appear at the far end. This is a complete cycle of subcarrier, or the whole colour spectrum and so cable length is extremely critical where colour phase is concerned. A 5° shift corresponds to the delay in just under a metre of cable.

There are other considerations. Consider two colours, one of low luminance, the other, high, present on the same line—a typical situation of adjacent scene colours. As the signal passes through apparatus, the colours may experience different degrees of distortion, which may alter their respective phase. Called differential phase distortion, NTSC has no way of remedying this. The colour burst has given the reference for that line; if the phase now alters during the line, it will be interpreted by the decoder as a change of hue.

PAL was developed to overcome these sorts of problems. It has an in-built protection to eliminate changes of hue arising from burst to chrominance phase errors. It is based on the principle of cancelling error by adding its opposite value. By switching the polarity of V (the red component axis) every line, any phase error apparent on one line will, in the next appear, as the opposite error. To the eye the two will cancel each other. The Appendix explains more about PAL. Perfection, however, is elusive. One can imagine that the eye will see the result of two opposing colours laid one over the other, as a reduction toward grey. In fact, desaturation does occur and if the phase error is great enough—right round by 180°—the colour will disappear entirely. But, for practical purposes, desaturation is to be preferred to colour change.

So how does NTSC deal with the problems of phase and timing? Simply by using good engineering design and maintenance standards, although, it must be said that when NTSC exhibits phase errors, they are most unpleasant. An indicator of how a practical system can fall short of the ideal.

In fact, since these systems were designed, technology has developed and improved so much that the protection afforded by PAL could be considered redundant. Well, this is an academic question; whilst a standard exists it has to be adhered to. But there is no doubt that PAL can and unfortunately does, encourage design 'corner cutting', particularly in some low-end systems.

The vectorscope

The vectorscope is really a precision composite video decoder with a vector display instead of a picture. It is similar in many ways to the waveform monitor but whereas the latter views linearly the vectorscope is rotary. The trace actually travels outwards from the centre to mark the colour vector positions. There is a rotary shift to align the display over the graticule and magnification to enlarge the trace so that low saturation colours can be observed—those that are very close to grey (or black or white). These will lie at or near the screen centre, which is zero colour (see Figure 5.9).

In addition to variable magnification, there is also provided 75% and 100% gain positions. These correspond to 75% and 100% colour bars, with the graticule markings, or boxes, for the fully saturated colours remaining the same. Both sets of bars will fall into these boxes when the appropriate gain is selected. The colour burst, however, has two marks for amplitude, as the burst remains the same at 0.3 Vpp, for both 75% and 100% colour bars.

Like the WFM there may be more than one input, allowing the display of more than one signal for comparison purposes. The instrument will lock to one or other signal. An external reference input is also provided, which can be either black and burst or any composite signal, the instrument will lock only to the colour burst.

Such is the basic hardware similarity between vectorscopes and WFMs that many manufacturers combine them into single units. The screen, CRT or other, is the same and switchable graticules are easy to provide. The combination offers lower overall cost and there is no serious disadvantage in this arrangement.

Vectorscopes and waveform monitors are complementary—neither can do the job of the other. In Part 2 we will see how the two work together.

The end of PAL and NTSC?

Composite video, it is often said, is nearing the end of its life. Digital installations and transmission is the new standard. Indeed they are.

For many years composite video has been the mainstay of television. In that time it has been both condemned for its degradation of picture quality, and at the same time, praised for its resilience. In this two factors are often overlooked. How the video signal has been 'squeezed' in the demand to cram more signal through the system. Bandwidth versus number of circuits, all boiling down to one common denominator: cost.

Both interlaced scanning and composite colour were invented to save bandwidth and reduce circuits. And—we must not forget—to fit the available technology of the time. But nowadays, we look back and see these innovations for what they were and call it 'compression'; the process of pruning a signal of its least significant parts to make it economical to transmit. Composite video is remarkable in squeezing colour into a one-circuit black and white system, but in doing so it does degrade. One cannot simply discard information and expect the effects of doing so never to show.

Interlace reduces vertical resolution, most noticeable in picture stills as an interline flutter of sharp horizontal edges. PAL and NTSC suffer from the interference with picture detail by the subcarrier.

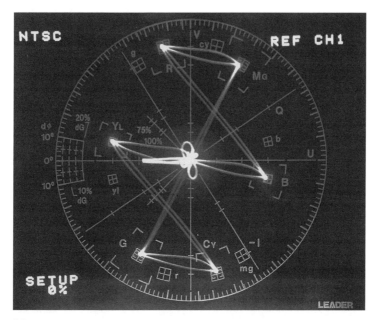

(a)

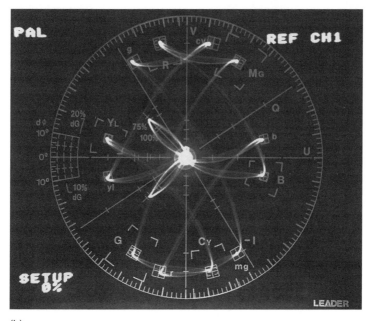

(b)

Figure 5.9   Vector display of colour bars. Vectors only show colour information; luminance values always appear as zero, i.e. the display centre. NTSC is shown in (a) and PAL in (b). Notice the effect of 180° subcarrier V phase change on alternate lines in PAL.

To fit into the existing bandwidth, the subcarrier had to be 'in-band', that is less than 5.5 MHz—rather less than the ideal 6.5 MHz calculated in Chapter 3. In-band subcarrier seriously compromises the finer scenic detail with objectionable 'cross colour' interference, particularly from woven fabric, where it is seen as a ringing pattern of colours. Reducing the effect means reducing the Y bandwidth even further making the picture less sharp.

PAL also suffers from its 'swinging red axis'. Introduced to remove phase errors, this operates over a two-line rate, giving rise to other implications (see Appendix).

Yet composite still lingers on. Many domestic receivers remain composite only. Yet, surprisingly, it is in monitoring, both picture and test and measurement, where PAL or NTSC may still persist. The principles are now so well established with WFMs and vectorscopes, and the many experienced users who seem reluctant to give them up even when this means coding to composite for this purpose alone.

Nowhere is this more evident than on location. While the signal may be digitised at the camera image sensors and pass to tape, or transmission, as a digital signal, the location picture monitor is often composite. Added to which may be a handy battery-operated test set of WFM and vectorscope, possibly Vical. Instruments which continue to give that all-important parameter: the confidence to say 'Yes ... the picture's good. Shoot it!'

The time is still some way away when camera and recorder manufacturers finally drop the composite output from its professional ranges. Paradoxically, it is the hi-end specs of modern video electronics that have honed composite to where it is now: still doing a useful job of work.

CHAPTER 6

NEW TECHNOLOGY

The shortcomings of composite video were put up with for as long as the single circuit remained the only option. It was known from the beginning that three circuits, either RGB or YUV, were the best method of sending colour video. Recording was the first to make the move. Magnetic tape has always been a serious bottle neck as regards the quest for quality, although this is in no way to deny the achievements of early tape or those who pursued its development. Composite recorders were huge machines. To size-down to more manageable proportions suitable for location shooting demanded a total reappraisal. There emerged the cassette based, time-multiplexed component recording systems based on component (luminance plus blue and red colour difference) signals. At a stroke, composite video was removed from the camera/recorder system (though it remained for monitoring). Sony Betacam SP was a leader in this field, soon to become world leader, such was its success.

However, in studios with ever-growing complexity, the single circuit and composite video remained.

Two-circuit component

At the same time, a variant of composite came about. A two-circuit technique of YC, luminance and chrominance, became a domestic, or low-end recording method, S-VHS is the typical example. The colour remains as a chrominance subcarrier, C, but as a separate signal and 'kept away' from the luminance to avoid side effects. Although aimed at non-broadcast markets, picture monitoring using YC has received a boost because it is a cost effective alternative to all-round digital monitoring. It is also provided for on many WFMs and vectorscopes.

The component standard

Before we venture further into the realm of digital video, we should pause to take one or two diversions to see the whole a little better. Not least that

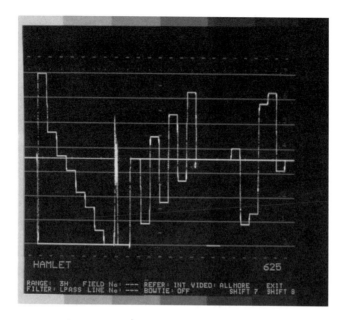

Figure 6.1 Component WFM showing colour bars. The waveform shows the three-signal display of 75% colour bars. The display is of luminance, followed by blue and red difference signals. Arranging the three signals one after the other is known as 'parade'. Compare with Figure 5.3. This particular waveform is derived from its digital equivalent and carries digital audio, which is the short pulse following the luminance component. Cr and Cb (R − Y and B − Y) are 75%.

important intermediate step which is the basis of modern digital video practice; component video, based on luminance and the two colour difference signals (see Figure 6.1). Note also how new terms have appeared; Cb is B − Y, and Cr is R − Y, and these must be distinguished from U and V, which are associated with PAL.

What is digital?

The traditional electric signal discussed so far in this book is analogue. Analogue replicates the original, and the signal so derived follows the form of light value or sound value, with time. Digitising is to give each amplitude value a number, which is then sent as a pulse code. Behind this lies the principle of binary maths.

Binary, as the term implies, is two-state. In electrical terms, a circuit is either on or off, which translates directly from the binary 0 or 1. We discussed two-state electric signals in Chapter 1 and saw how simple they were. Except that now, the speed must increase far beyond hand operation of a key,

Table 6.1 Binary series

Quantization value	Circuit A	Circuit B	Circuit C
1	0	0	0
2	0	0	1
3	0	1	0
4	0	1	1
5	1	0	0
6	1	0	1
7	1	1	0
8	1	1	1

to … well, suffice to say, sending a code describing some hundreds of levels at pixel rate, or 800 times per line, is very fast indeed. But the essence of simplicity remains.

Conversion works like this. The most significant bit is determined by whether the signal exceeds 50% or not. If it does, next determine whether it exceeds 75%—that's the next bit. If it does not reach 50%, does it get to 25%? And so on. This principle of breaking every part of the signal into bits is called 'quantising', or the action of determining pixel value, and a number is allocated to the bit series so derived. This is the basis of digital signals.

Binary numbers are to the base 2, that is they only count up to two, the numbers are zero and one, hence the 0s and 1s used in digital language. A simple binary series that will count up to 8 requires three circuits and is shown in Table 6.1. Eight bits means that the system can distinguish eight individual levels of signal.

Three circuits are required to carry this amount of data. Circuit A carries the most significant bit, Circuit B the next, Circuit C carries the least significant bit. Loss of the circuit carrying the least significant bit is the least disruptive but loss of Circuit A would be catastrophic.

Converting from analogue to digital means that the picture is subjected to amplitude measurement at a pixel rate and the value of each pixel converted to a number (shown in Figure 6.2). The critical part of the digital system is the conversion process—a process that must be carried out at a rate at least twice that of the highest frequency of the signal.

Every level is given a binary number and if we require 100 levels, a figure based on a tonal resolution between black and white of 100 levels would take seven circuits. In fact, 100 levels are inconvenient; if we do the binary arithmetic, we find the number comes out at 128. Digital video began with an 8 bit system giving 256 levels, although only 235 are available to picture information. The current standard is now 10 bit and offers almost 1000 levels of quantisation. At, or near, black level this degree of tonal resolution is very

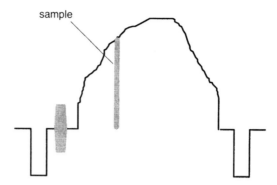

Figure 6.2   Sampling the waveform. The waveform level is measured at the sampling rate, which is pixel size. Each level is given a binary number. There will be as many binary numbers as there are pixels. The sampling rate is fixed by the number of pixels per second.

important if picture content and colour are to be reproduced accurately in these dark areas.

Figure 6.2 shows a line of composite video. Digitising PAL or NTSC involves a sampling rate as it is known, four times the subcarrier frequency (17.7 MHz for PAL, 14.3 for NTSC) if the colour subcarrier is to be analysed correctly, thus demanding a four-fold increase of bandwidth. Although some fine tuning of sampling frequency can be done, digitising still places greater demands on available signal space.

Digitised or not, composite video is what it is; a three-signal band-limited signal squeezed into one. While composite still performs a service, digital composite has, in most cases, already passed its day.

4:2:2 … and all that!

We now often see the term '4:2:2' used in connection with component or component digital video. It is derived from the three-colour system and is used as an indicator of quality standard. We saw in Chapter 5 how colour in RGB form required full bandwidth circuits for all three colours, as each carried a proportion of luminance information. On the other hand, converting RGB to YCbCr (Y, B − Y, R − Y) concentrated the luminance information, with all its demands for picture sharpness, into one circuit, Y. Now Cb and Cr no longer need the bandwidth of Y, and the difference is about 2:1. Hence, we can say that if each circuit of RGB is given a value of 4, then Cb and Cr will be 2.

From this a family of quality values has emerged. For instance, 4:1:1 relates to the lower colour difference bandwidths of the PAL U and V signals. These terms may appear arbitrary (numeral '4' originally relates to 4 × NTSC subcarrier frequency) but they have become established into common use.

Why digital?

One overriding reason. In the digital domain the signal is extremely well protected from distortion or interference. The digital signal is no more than 0s and 1s, two levels only and, as long as the detection system can distinguish a 0 from a 1, the system will function. Video tape, noisy circuits, no longer have the disastrous effect they would once have had. Systems no longer need to operate from DC to the highest frequency, but may be designed to function at far higher, but as very narrow bands of frequencies. Cable costs are reduced. Fibre links—modulating the signal onto light and sending along cables of glass fibre—can carry many times more information than traditional copper ones. Interference from all kinds of sources and operating conditions will be ignored by the digital process.

One of the driving forces to go digital was the newly developing graphics industry servicing TV production and advertising. Computers revolutionised the manipulation of stills, much of which was directly applicable to television. Moving graphics followed not long after. Many of the standards for digital video stemmed from the development of computer graphics.

And nor must the growing art of digital video effects be ignored. Picture manipulation is the other side of digital operations, and readily lends itself to the process. While once this was the domain of mainframe computing, today the power of the modern PC permits its integration into production and transmission operations. Also, the use of different aspect ratios (widths of picture) are more easily accommodated as pixel sizes and counts can be altered more easily, both at source and display.

The synchroniser

At this stage it's worth looking at the synchroniser. Historically, the synchroniser's appearance heralded the digital era. Put simply, it is a box with a video input and video output, and a memory between. Memory—or the means to hold in electronic store—was virtually impossible in analogue form. Only magnetic tape could record and hold a signal, then play back again. But tape degraded, and speed of access to the signal was limited by how fast the mechanics could spool and search.

However, the arrival of digits made possible a store which would not degrade the signal and with sufficient access speed to offer real-time processing. The memory could hold a complete frame. Video goes in and one frame later it appears at the output. Therefore a whole frame is stored inside, constantly moving through but a complete $\frac{1}{25}$ second worth of video nonetheless. Using a time reference—the ubiquitous genlock—to control when the signal is released from the store, it is possible to synchronise any source whatever it is or where. The output appears the same as the input for the device is essentially transparent. Apart, that is, from the timing change, or delay. A synchroniser is passive—it can only delay.

A synchroniser can make up for clock rate differences, meaning that a distant source without any timing reference to the mixing point whatsoever can be made synchronous. In doing so the signal is delayed by up to one frame. Such a delay is in itself of no importance, but one must consider the other element of the remote source: audio. Audio sent over conventional circuits will, of course, not be subject to timing delays; it will therefore arrive before the video. One twenty-fifth of a second may not seem much, but where multiple synchronisers are used in a transmission chain, lip-sync errors may appear. Audio delays have been introduced to overcome the problem.

The timing controls are H, horizontal or line phase, and C, colour phase, for the original synchronisers were designed for composite video. There are additional signal level controls as well: gain, lift (the engineering term is preferred to pedestal) and colour saturation.

While synchronisers were used initially for distant sources, their versatility developed with technology to where they are now: integral with other parts of the programme chain, as we shall see later.

Sending digits

When first describing the video signal and how it is transmitted, one option (set out way back in Figure 3.3) was to send each pixel along its own circuit—an impracticable option because of the circuit complexity. Here we have a similar situation with each data bit allocated a circuit of its own. This is termed parallel data and is shown in Figure 6.3. There was also the more practical method of Figure 3.4, and we can see its similarity to Figure 6.4 where the signal is digitised into a bit stream and sent down a single circuit as serial data. The penalty is that the data rate has to increase in order to transfer the same amount of data in real, or picture time.

The data rate will depend on how fast the signal can be sampled and what level of accuracy is required. Going back once more, telegraphy used a data rate that worked at human operator speed, fitting the cable technology of the day. If we want to send digital video at this speed we could do so but would have to reduce the frame rate such that the signal would appear as a sequence of stills, probably no faster than one a week. Alternatively, we could trade picture quality for speed.

Consider now how component video is handled. The Y signal's highest frequency is 5.5 MHz and, unlike composite sampling at four times colour subcarrier, the finest scene detail requires at least two-times sampling.

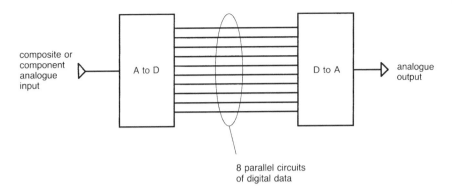

Figure 6.3 Parallel digital circuit. The analogue to digital converter produces an 8-bit parallel output. At the destination the reverse takes place.

This means the electronics operate twice as fast as in conventional video and will use twice the bandwidth.

Packaging video into a digital form demands that another standard be created. Standard ITU-R BT.601 (the earlier US standard is SMPTE ANSI 125M) is based on component video, Y, R − Y, B − Y (more commonly now seen written in the form YCbCr). One of the aims of the 601 standard was to be applicable to both European 625/50 and American 525/60 standards. The sampling rate for Y is 13.5 MHz and 6.75 MHz for Cr and Cb, resulting in serial data rate of 270 Mbits/s (megabits/second). So we begin to see how much more demanding digital video can be of circuit bandwidth. But it is a single circuit with—as far as that is possible—original source picture quality. And the standard also caters for digital audio and other information as well.

It is the act of conversion that is most demanding. The conversions, analogue to digital and back again, are where the signal is most vulnerable to error. Measuring discrete levels means that approximations are made.

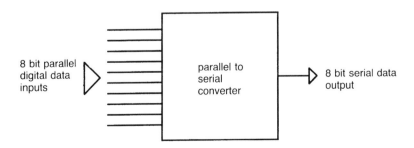

Figure 6.4 Parallel to serial conversion. Eight wires down to a single wire. The data rate has to go up by eight times in the series circuit, requiring eight times the bandwidth.

Take those near to black; distinguishing between 0 and 1% is far more significant than distinguishing between 99% and 100%. Yet the digitising system will give equal emphasis to both.

The effect is due to quantising the levels as discrete steps, a situation improved by increasing the number of bits. A one-bit system can only distinguish two levels and the quantising distortion will reduce the image to only two tones. Using 100 levels, at or near black, quantising distortion will be evident under good viewing conditions as discrete tones rather than the smooth gradation of the original analogue signal. It is a matter of choice; to decide how good the tonal resolution must be for a practical system.

From this it would seem that the action of digitising a signal and back again, will inevitably distort it. Well, it does. Digital signals are not free from errors. So it is highly desirable to avoid needless conversion and reconversion. Once converted to digital, as early as possible, it should remain in the digital domain as long as possible. Ideally, right up to the very end of the chain at the picture display.

Video is more forgiving than audio in this respect because the number of levels, or bits, required for video pictures is less than hi-fi audio. The audio dynamic range we hear is many times greater than the video contrast range. As with any system, care must always be exercised over the design and usage of equipment if we are to benefit fully from the advantages of digital video production.

Whereas analogue will, if the signs of signal degradation are read properly by those watching, give some warning of pending problems, digital will not. By its very construction it will ignore all the major factors that affect the analogue signal, until in the end it is too late. When the digital destination is unable to make sense of the signal because it has become so corrupted or obscured, the result is total collapse. A digital signal is vulnerable in this one respect, and its consequences are sudden and catastrophic... likened to the crash so often talked about where computers are concerned. But even this, in terms of signal degradation, is orders of magnitude better than would be acceptable in any analogue system.

To read the signal, the digital to analogue converter must be able to do two things: to know which part of the signal is which, and to be able to interpret the bit code. To do so it must be able to synchronise itself to the incoming data stream. If it fails to hold synchronism because of noise interference, corruption will occur.

Should the digital signal become corrupted, for instance, a bit is missing, then the system can be made self-checking and compensation put in place. In a practical system, it is quite reasonable to expect a bit to become corrupted every so often because of noise or interference. Video tape is a good example. An automatic monitor that can spot the problem can also make a good guess at what the faulty sample should have been. It has only to look at those either side and average to get the answer.

The conversion back to analogue should ideally be as close to the end of the chain as possible. But by this time the signal will have passed through considerable processing and routeing systems over various circuits to arrive at its destination. Every stage is a potential source of noise and corruption but with good design and proper usage, digital processing is, on balance, still able to offer much greater flexibility.

Measurement of digital video

Placing the signal into digital form does not remove the measuring requirement. Inside its digital package, there is still the original signal that must comply with the original standard. It must not exceed the maximum of white at 100% or 0.7 V above black, and must not go below black. Colour too, must likewise comply with the standard maximum defined by colour bars.

As regards measurement, what has been described so far about WFMs still applies. An analogue WFM can be used before digitisation, or a digital WFM afterwards. However, once coded into digital form the signal is fixed, and to correct or alter it will involve either conversion back to analogue, or to use digital equipment designed for that purpose. Should the signal be distorted before digitising, or by the action of digitising because it lies outside the standard, it may be impossible to put right.

In practice we would find it impracticable to use a standard WFM on a digital circuit to look at the raw data, and make any kind of sense of what we see. To the eye, the waveform of a binary number is a meaningless array of pulses unless we introduce specialised techniques. Automatic monitoring of the data stream with equipment that is able to analyse and indicate the state of the signal is the only practical way. The whole test and measurement operation is in digital form—there is no need to convert to analogue—the monitor simply looks at the data and interprets into a display. The result is a read-out, either as 'yes/no' indication, or, if the waveform is relevant, to display in that form. In either case, it is the user's choice.

Here we are bound by the needs of the operator. The digital signal is a very complex one. There are many parameters that need to be monitored. And as always, different operators will expect different facilities and different information from their test and measurement. Some are interested only in the picture, others are more engineering based. Figure 6.5 shows an example of a very simple device.

There is now a wide variety of test gear available with as wide a variation in pricing. In each case we are bound by how an individual item evaluates and what emphasis it places on signal parameters. Digital video gives no option but to rely on such equipment. It should be remembered though, digital systems, whether signal processing or monitoring, are on the whole, reliable—a feature that directly stems from the two-state binary operation.

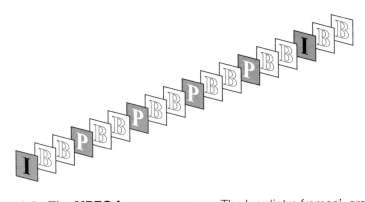

Figure 6.6 The MPEG frame sequence. The I, or 'intra frames', are non-compressed reference frames. The P frames, or 'predictive frames', having moderate compression, enable the heavily compressed B, or 'bidirectional frames', to be reconstructed. This MPEG example is the 15 frame version used for the USA 525 line video standard (525/29.97 or 525/59.94). It repeats every 0.5 seconds. 625 line video (625/25 or 625/50) has a 12 video frame sequence.

Such a long video frame sequence makes cutting and mixing difficult. Breaking the sequence requires re-coding the frames either side of the break with attendant degradation. But as most production facilities function pre-MPEG coding, such constraints will not normally arise. Where tapes or other media are created in MPEG, then the sequence must be observed when setting up the editing system. MPEG 2 is therefore a useful transmission and storage standard but is more limited in video effects and editing operations.

Alternative profiles of MPEG 2 have been introduced to offset some of these shortcomings. Future variants will continue to appear as new demands are made and the technology continues to advance.

There are other compression standards created by manufacturers for their own systems. A camera and recorder, or camcorder, may use compression specific to that design. Whilst that is perfectly legitimate in the confines of the camera, where that material is required to integrate with other compression formats the resulting artefacts could interact with unpredictable results.

The quest for quality

Great emphasis is placed on the quality of digital signals. In reality, these are only as good as the source material and it is therefore gratifying that signal acquisition has made significant advances as well. Where digitised signals score so dramatically is because of their immunity to signal recording and processing distortion that has so plagued analogue.

As long as the digital system is correctly designed, installed and maintained to its specification it will always appear transparent, and this should be allowed to remain its major strength.

The subject of wide screen is also part of the quality issue. Strictly, widening the picture demands more pixels if the same resolution based on viewing distance and picture height are to be adhered to. A sampling frequency of 18 MHz would be required for an aspect ratio of 16:9, which is outside the digital standard. Wide screen, therefore, makes use of 'wide pixels', the same number per line as before, but stretched out. Despite the corresponding loss of horizontal resolution, the effect on quality is not as significant as one might imagine. This technique is now incorporated into the 601 standard, although not widely used.

Part Two

In Practice

CHAPTER 7

FIRST STEPS—THE CAMERA

We have discussed at length the background to video signals and measurement. Now is the time to look at practical situations. First there are the picture sources and then, how these link into systems. The most complex picture source is the camera because unlike any other, its output is photographic and is therefore unpredictable as regards tonal range and colour. But before we lose ourselves in the excitement of the camera, we must first deal with another aspect of the video system.

Terminations

Chapter 1 laid the groundwork to understanding sources, circuits and destinations, and described the principles of sending and receiving video signals.

The standard video connector is the BNC, a bayonet locking connector that preserves the circuit characteristic right through from cable to equipment. Proper termination is necessary to ensure the transmission of a video signal along a cable of any length with minimum loss and distortion. As part of this design standard, the source must be correctly loaded, or terminated. Only when this is done will the signal appear at its destination at the correct level and with minimum distortion.

Figure 7.1 illustrates a common problem: one source, one destination. Video is a complex waveform that requires correctly designed circuits to comply with the standard of one source for one destination. Every source, whether camera, video tape player, or test signal generator, may only feed one destination. Where sources have more than one output, each output will be isolated from the others, so becoming a separate source in its own right. For this reason it is common practice to have more than one output. Many lightweight cameras have only a single composite output. This is intended for monitoring but will be in most cases to broadcast specification and so may be used as main output if composite is the required format. But how is the problem posed in Figure 7.1 dealt with?

(a)

(b)

Figure 7.3　Distortion due to incorrect termination. When camera and monitor are properly set up and the signal correctly terminated, the picture will appear as in (a). When unterminated the result will be as in (b). Reducing monitor contrast will make the picture seem correct; the fault, however, will remain on the recording.

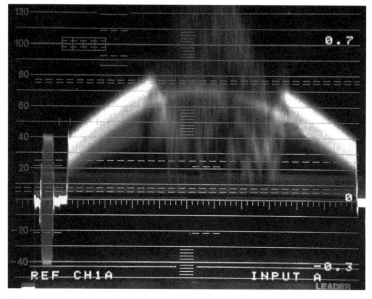

(a)

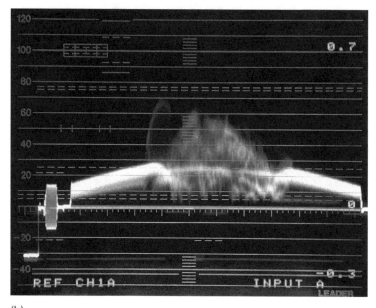

(b)

Figure 7.4   Waveforms of incorrect terminations. (a) The signal is unterminated and the amplitude is twice that of a terminated signal, resulting in signal levels well beyond the permitted maximum of 100% or 0.7 V. The signal is double terminated in (b) and the amplitude is reduced by a third.

A broadcast, or equivalent camera has a 'colour bars' function. Whenever a recording is made, or a signal sent by any other means, it is convention for a half-minute or so of colour bars to precede the pictures. They will be accepted as representing the maximum values of all the colour signal parameters at the destination and will be used to set up receiving apparatus, video tape players and so on. Your pictures must therefore conform to the standard and, generally speaking, camera design ensures that this is so.

Select 'Colour Bars' on the camera. As the standard test signal, colour bars may be relied upon to conform to the video standard but we will check that this is so. Looking at colour bars on a picture monitor will prove very little about how accurate the bars are. A WFM is essential to check out colour bars, and a vectorscope as well if available.

In Chapter 5, we learned what colour bars are and how they are generated. Connect the WFM to the camera output—not forgetting the termination. You will find the WFM handbook helpful here if the unit's back panel labelling isn't. Connect a picture monitor as well, looping through to the WFM to ensure proper termination. It is all too easy to disregard the picture when carrying out engineering checks. Learn to relate the waveforms to the pictures they represent, which is so very important if a full and rounded knowledge of video is to be acquired.

With all connections in place, there should be a display of 75% colour bars, as in Figure 7.7. If the waveform shows 100% bars the fact should be noted as such because 100% bars is not an acceptable test signal in certain circumstances.

Check the level of the white bar is at 100% or 0.7 V above black level. The syncs are 0.3 V below black level and the colour burst is 0.3 Vpp. Once more, NTSC and PAL throw up another subtle difference, this time relating to the ratio of picture to sync amplitudes. NTSC sync and burst are not quite 0.3 V. The Appendix has the details.

All this amounts to a check of the composite output of the camera whilst the recorder will invariably be taking the signal in component or digital component form. But in doing this we have proved a large chunk of the signal path. To complete the test, record a half-minute of colour bars and look at these played back.

Some older camcorders may not playback all that well, providing low-quality pictures for basic monitoring only. Refer to the manual if in doubt. If the playback is not good enough to prove the recording, it may be necessary to transfer the tape to a full specification machine.

Should any deviation be noted from the correct colour bar form, the situation should be dealt with by a qualified engineer. It is unlikely that adjustment will be available without dismantling the camera. What degree of error is acceptable depends entirely on the circumstances of the camera's use. An analogue system may show a slight variation from the original recorded version. This is quite normal. A digital playback should be indistinguishable from the original.

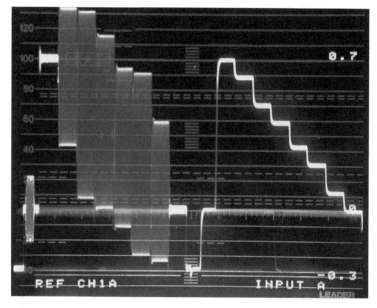

(a)

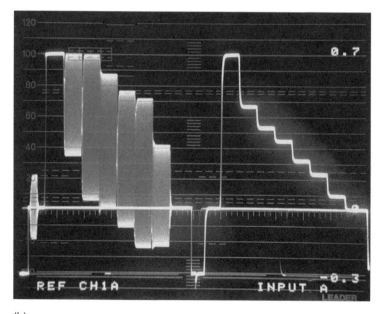

(b)

Figure 7.7 100% and 75% colour bars. 100% colour bars are shown in (a) and 75% colour bars in (b). Both displays show full composite and luminance only using the 'parade' function. Note how the luminance values differ between the 100% and 75% versions.

)ption to set pedestal wherever one wants does present the risk of ₀₋tting it wrong. Whilst discussing the faults arising from setting it too low, we must not overlook the consequences of too high a setting. Increasing pedestal raises black to grey, softening contrast and offering a very useful pictorial device if that is what is wanted. But it does reduce the available picture contrast range. Hence, a setting of 3% is a good all-round figure for most work. Many photographers prefer to alter contrast by optical filtration, leaving pedestal alone and so avoiding the risk of getting it wrong. It is to be hoped, however, that better understanding will bring about more willingness to use this valuable control for entirely pictorial effect.

Measuring 3% may not be found easy. It is a very small increment to see on a WFM; some instruments may have the means to measure such small values, but many may not. The Vical method, discussed later, is designed with this in mind, but for the moment let us see what 3% actually means. It corresponds to 21 mV (0.021 V) and guessing so small a level is probably the best one can aim for with a conventional waveform display. In fact, the actual figure is of less interest, it is far more important to have camera black *above* 0%. It is only when we work with more than one camera that greater precision is required in the matching of one camera pedestal to another. But that's yet another topic for later.

The Appendix has further information on contrast values that will be useful in comparing percentage to voltage levels.

Having checked out colour bars and ascertained the pedestal level, we have completed a major part of the camera check-out. Many more parameters remain in the camera; some will not be possible to deal with in a simple procedure but as the process unfolds, various observations can be made that will provide a very useful measure of confidence in the camera's performance. Now we can look at the picture.

The picture

There's no apologies for the diversion that now follows. When using a picture monitor it is imperative that you have confidence in it. The monitor must be in subdued light, although the scene or check-out chart for the camera must be well lit. If you cannot see the picture reliably there is little point in having it, for it will only mislead and confuse.

The principle controls on the monitor are brightness and contrast. A simple test to prove how important it is to get these correct is to increase camera pedestal and then reduce monitor brightness and see how one cancels the other. It is this sort of confusion that has caused problems over pedestal setting. A similar interaction exists between camera iris and contrast.

There is no reliable answer to this without the introduction of monitor set-up equipment. If such is available, make use of it. The Appendix describes two such pieces of equipment. Alternatively, many modern monitors address the problem by having preset positions for the controls but even here, there is no allowance for variation in viewing conditions. Nor can we exclude the possibility that preset controls may have been disturbed. Such is the precision required in monitor set-up that many modern monitors have concealed controls, yet even here it is only right that we should satisfy ourselves. The importance of accurate picture monitoring cannot be over emphasised. The procedure described will concentrate on setting brightness and contrast.

When black is sent, black should be seen—a contradiction in itself. It is 'the seeing of black' that causes the difficulty. Capping the camera means that camera pedestal, which is picture black, appears on the screen. Raise the monitor brightness until this becomes grey, then reduce until black. Having discussed the careful setting of pedestal, such a method of setting monitor brightness is similarly far too inaccurate.

Colour bars offer nothing in this regard; the signal has no elements able to provide even the roughest guide to brightness setting. What is required is a method that takes into account the individuality of picture monitors and, most important, the viewing conditions. Such is only possible with a picture set-up test signal. Picture line-up generators are available that produce a signal based on a black ground with patches at various levels from 5% to 100%. Brightness is set so that black and 5% are just resolved, whilst the light output from the 100% white can be measured and contrast adjusted as per the monitor manual.

The Vical method is designed specifically for the single camera and monitor situation. It works by inserting a test signal into the camera signal. Vical is connected between camera and monitor and a three-step pattern of 0% black, a variable level grey, and 100% white, are inserted into the camera output and displayed on the monitor as part of the camera signal. With the camera capped, brightness may now be very accurately set by observing the difference between the video black from Vical and camera pedestal. Vical is described in more detail later.

Whichever method is chosen to set up the picture, make sure it is used properly. Before we look at the camera's picture, there are a couple of quick observations to be done with the lens capped. When no light enters the camera, there should be no output. Ideals are rarely achieved and the camera invariably produces some spurious signal where there should be nothing, particularly with older models. Raise the monitor brightness until the camera black appears as dark grey. Remember, this is the camera pedestal; also remember what black is—it's no colour, with red, green and blue at zero. On our monitor what we see may not be quite so perfect. Look carefully for changes in brightness and colour, but you must keep the screen dark to do so.

If after a little careful study you do see imperfections, possibly shading in colour or luminance, look at the WFM. Can you relate the two displays? Look for tiny specks in the picture, usually white; these are where the CCD sensor chip has 'drop out', caused by faulty pixels. Another is colour shading,

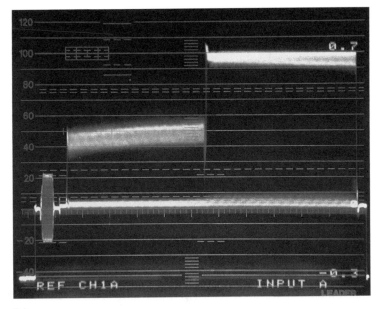

(b)

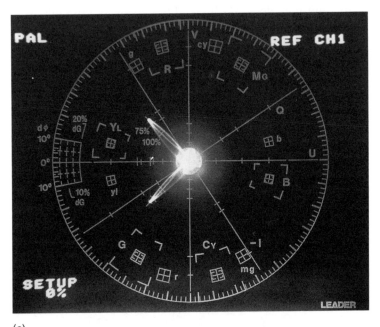

(c)

Figure 7.9b,c (continued) Grey and white cards. The waveform is shown in (b). The camera is exposed to bring the white card to 100%; the grey card level reads 40%. Note that the waveform level is not consistent because of the variation in light level across the cards. The picture does not reveal this so easily—an instance of where the WFM tells more than the picture. The vectorscope display in (c) is at the centre showing that no colour is present.

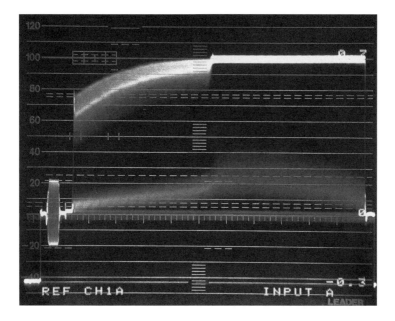

Figure 7.10 Peak white clipping. The camera is over-exposed and the white card is clipped back to 100%. Compare this with Figure 7.9(b).

Contrast control is possible in various ways to alleviate the problem of excessive scene contrast. Signal level will be subject to compression as it approaches 100%, controlling the higher picture tones. Peak white clipping still takes place at 100%, but its effect will be less obvious to the eye. Figure 7.11 shows how contrast control operates.

Contrast control may be seen working when the camera points at a white card, it may not permit exposure of the fully framed white to 100%. The effect may be even more pronounced with dynamic contrast control (DCC). DCC continuously adjusts as scene content changes: it may reveal itself as allowing white speculas to reach 100% but holding down broader areas of white to below that limit. Therefore, when conducting the tests described here, the contrast control, or DCC, is best switched off. Dynamic contrast control methods are generally much more sophisticated than a static arrangement but the option to switch off may still be useful in certain instances. The camera's manual should explain the specific methods used.

Colour balance

Readjust the camera for correct exposure with the white card at 100% (but not clipped). White has no colour, nor has grey, and the waveforms should show no evidence of subcarrier. Subcarrier will be present where there is

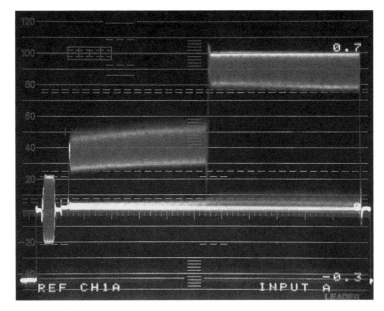

(a)

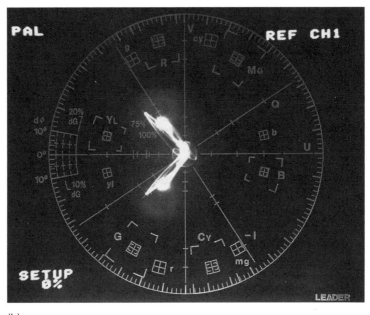

(b)

Figure 7.12   Camera white balance error. The white balance is incorrect and the grey cards are not reproduced as grey and chrominance is present. It appears on the WFM (a) as subcarrier and causes a thickening of the trace. The vectorscope (b) shows the colour as a shift away from the centre of the display on the red/yellow axis. Compare with Figure 7.9.

To measure sensitivity requires knowing the level of light reaching the camera lens. The lens iris, or aperture, is calibrated in f-stops. Changing the iris by one stop alters the light transmission by a factor of 2 (see the Appendix for more information). Sensitivity is calibrated in lens f-stop for a given light level. The value of this is to be able to compare one camera to another. Although a camera's ability to function in low light is desirable, it does not preclude the photographic skill of the operator in using light creatively to produce fine pictures. That is required whatever the camera.

An indication of correct exposure is provided in the viewfinder and known as 'zebra'. The name originates from the form of the diagonal moving pattern that appears when picture elements reach a specific level. Measuring this is part of the check-out procedure. Switch on zebra if not already done, and increase camera exposure. As the white card rises in level, zebra pattern will appear in those areas exceeding a predetermined value. Further increase eventually raises the grey card to the same level and that too becomes subject to the zebra pattern. Reducing exposure causes the pattern to disappear. Note the level on the waveform at which zebra appears, making sure that you identify the correct point by relating picture to waveform. Measure the level on the waveform.

The point at which zebra appears is adjustable and a personal choice. It is also influenced by the actual method utilised in any particular camera. A good guide figure is 90% for this will alert you to levels approaching 100%.

Camera sensitivity is variable in steps, sometimes called gain and occasionally sensitivity. The calibration is in decibels, abbreviated to dBs, or may be expressed as a factor. Sensitivity, in stops of exposure, is a direct relation to the rating of photographic film. Gain and sensitivity are related thus:

DBs	-6	0	6	9	12	18
Gain (factor)	$\times 0.5$	$\times 1.0$	$\times 2.0$	$\times 3.0$	$\times 4.0$	$\times 8.0$
Sensitivity (f-stops)	-1	0	$+1$	$+1\frac{1}{2}$	$+2$	$+3$

Modern CCD cameras have variable shutters, which may be mechanical or electronic. They arise from the need to shutter the light from the sensor during its read-out time and are now adopted as an operational feature. The camera shutter sets the exposure time. The original tube cameras exposed at $1/25$ second per frame but for CCDs this is now more usually $1/50$ s or $1/60$ s. The exposure at other shutter timings are:

Shutter exposure (seconds)	$\frac{1}{50}$	$\frac{1}{125}$	$\frac{1}{250}$	$\frac{1}{500}$	$\frac{1}{1000}$
Relative exposure (f-stops)	0	-1	-2	-3	-4

The presence of $1/60$ s shutter is so similar to $1/50$ s as to make little practical difference to exposure.

It is worth considering the form of graticule scale used on the WFM. We have described signal level in two ways: picture levels are more meaningful in

effect as described in Figure 7.11. This causes the higher tones to compress in rather a similar way to low gamma, although knee does not alter tones below about 85%. So the two effects can be rather similar and must not be confused.

Working with a high gamma—setting the grey card to give 40% while white remains at 100%—has value for the more dramatic shots. Colour saturation will also increase in dark tones so beware that facial shadows do not become too florid, unless of course, this is the way you want your pictures to look.

Colorimetry

Colorimetry used to be an absolute—a 'no touch' parameter from the early days of television. It was never an easy-to-measure kind of control because colour co-ordinates were designed very carefully and specific to the colour splitting optics used in each camera design. However, the menu control of a modern digital camera makes this adjustment less forbidding, but it is still most important to know what you're trying to achieve. Read the manual: gain some insight into how the camera functions. Find out about colorimetry... there's a brief overview in the Appendix. This is not as straightforward a control as the others we have talked about.

One or two general rules ...

If a control is offered as a user-set facility it's meant to be used, but...

- understand what a control does before you disturb it;
- make sure you are able to restore it to its original position;
- and remember... there are many controls inside cameras, particularly older ones, that are very definitely engineering. If in doubt... don't touch!

Menus and digital cameras

In going through this procedure, we have checked the most significant parts of the camera. It may seem to some rather scant. There is a reason. What has been dealt with here is the basic camera system and modern cameras do not lend themselves to over-zealous tweaking. Just like their forbears, they need to be understood and worked on with care. And that starts with the basics.

One of the most innovative developments is the menu control through software of all the camera's parameters. The facility first appeared on cameras when digital processing was introduced to control the parameters of the analogue circuits—with the designer thoughtfully providing a reset action to put everything back to factory settings.

There is little point in having any facility unless one is able to properly assess each change as it is made, which means understanding the picture. It's all down to experience; there's no short cut. Unless, that is, you are always willing to reset and return to the camera's own ideas about how your pictures should look.

When considering alternative methods of video measurement in a later chapter, the Vical method is described which uses visual techniques to compare tonal and colour balance against a known reference. This picture-oriented technique was created to fill the gap between the graphical wave-form and the pure picture and provides simple measurement without its user ever becoming detached from the picture. It therefore is an alternative tool of learning for those who want to find out about signals and video from the pictorial—and proper—standpoint.

The fact is that all measurement methods have their limitations: WFMs, reference picture monitors and specialist devices; each has its own virtues and its own shortcomings. Neither will on its own completely satisfy all the needs of comprehensive video measurement. Photography, which is the backbone of video, is a combination of artistic and craft skills that we all must learn to channel into the available technology.

A footnote ...

It will not have passed unnoticed that most of our discussion has revolved around composite video. In this burgeoning digital world the author makes no apology for this; there still exists—and we will see more of it yet—the established and proven standard of composite and the single circuit. There remains a place for this outdated modus operandi because of one specific: composite monitoring. Study the following examples in Figure 7.13 to see how the signal flow has evolved and the implications arising. While NTSC and PAL are offered as outputs on so many kinds of camera—not only movie but still as well—then we will see composite monitoring being offered to make use of it. And we must not lose sight of the fact that composite video has benefited from the same technological advances that have been made on behalf of its successors.

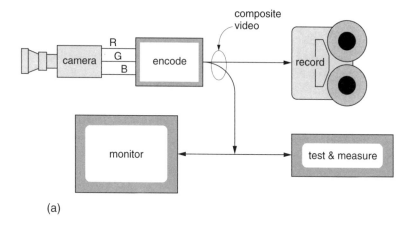

(a)

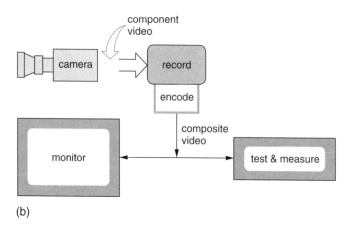

(b)

Figure 7.13a,b   Single camera to recorder. (a) *Composite camera*: The system is composite from the camera back onwards. The camera processes in RGB or Y, R − Y, B − Y, and encodes into composite for recording and monitoring. (b) *Component camera*: The camera processes in RGB or Y, R − Y, B − Y component, the latter passes to the recorder and is also encoded into composite for monitoring.

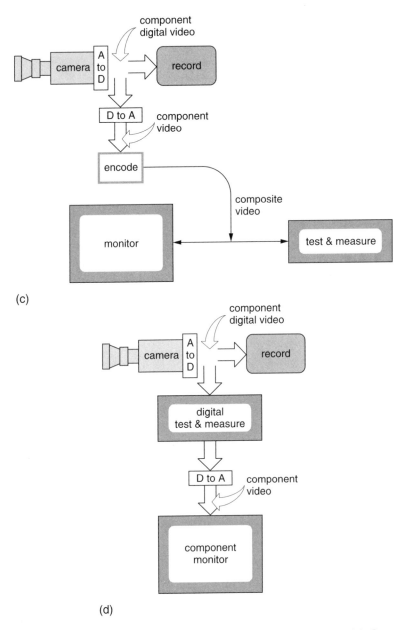

(c)

(d)

Figure 7.13c,d (continued) Single camera to recorder. (c) *Component digital camera*: This is a common digital set up. The analogue signal off the image sensors is converted to digital, allowing full digital signal processing all the way to the recording medium and beyond. To accommodate composite monitoring, the digital signal (after camera processing) must be converted to analogue component then encoded into composite. (d) Similar to (c) but with digital component monitoring Digital test and measurement and component monitoring eliminates composite entirely. The viewer, however, may still require composite and ideally, digital to analogue conversion and encoding into PAL or NTSC should take place as late in the chain as possible.

CHAPTER 8

THE STUDIO

The previous chapter described the basic camera system and its set up. Now we shall extend this into studio multi-camera operation, plus other sources such as graphics and caption generators. These are typical studio facilities requiring level set-up and timing.

Signal levels

Picture levels may exceed the standard limits as described in Chapter 7. A camera may be able to handle an extended scene contrast range that reproduces as an extended video signal. Levels as high as 125% are not unknown. Where shooting conditions are not fully controllable in exterior locations with bright clouds in blue skies, extended contrast is an advantage. Modern CCD image sensors have a wide contrast acceptance and the signal processing is designed accordingly.

Where such programme material remains local and unlikely to pass through international circuits, such high levels may be permissible. But it must always be remembered that these signals are not legitimate and if sent through equipment complying with international standards such excesses will be removed. Brilliant skies, subtle reflections and speculas that offer so much to the creative eye, may easily exceed the 1 V maximum. Niceties wasted, cut back to 100% and lost, never to be seen by client or viewer.

Peak white clipping normally takes place at the main studio output as part of the compliance with the video standard. It is worth checking out cameras to see if they exceed peak white, a procedure described in Chapter 7.

If pictures are allowed to exceed 100%, the whole principle of a 100% test signal is rather pointless. The presence of colour bars at the start of a recording implies that 100% is the maximum. It is confusing to those receiving your programme if your colour bars are not representative of the picture levels that follow. The recipient would be perfectly entitled to accept the colour bars as correct and allow the removal of any excess over 100%. This applies in real-time programmes as well as recorded material. Better the limit be applied at the shooting stage, unless you are lucky enough to see your pictures right through post-production and properly graded. But that's another issue. It remains for you, as the programme originator, to control your pictures and you must be prepared to work within the video standard.

Checking colour bars, as previously described, is part of programme origination. It is also part of programme transmission. Colour bars may appear in either 75% or 100% form in production areas. The 100% version is unacceptable to many transmission systems and it is therefore important to ascertain which version is appropriate to your operation.

Timing

In checking out the camera we made no mention of 'time'. Timing is a relative parameter and, for an isolated picture source, is irrelevant; the picture display(s) are simply slaved to follow the picture source. However, a studio with more than one source, has a timing requirement. The pictures must arrive in synchronism at the mixing or switching point if picture disturbances are to be avoided when selecting one source after another. Sources may be routed through diverging signal paths, through various video effects, but must all arrive together at the same point in time. Those with longer paths must start earlier.

If pictures are to be mixed and inlaid together, they must be synchronised very accurately to ensure the picture elements register. When synchronism is achieved, a whole variety of picture effects and manipulation is possible; the output, however, always maintains an unbroken sync pulse sequence.

Getting all the sources to arrive in sync at the mixer requires genlock. Each source must have the same picture starting point and to do so, its scan timing generator must be locked to all other generators. The simplest method is for one source to be master and slave the others to its output. A video input, called 'genlock', is provided on most cameras and other picture generators for the purpose. Whilst this is perfectly acceptable technically, it is not always convenient to use a picture source, and more usually a dedicated source of genlock from a sync pulse generator is used instead. The SPG, as it is known, is a reliable and permanent sync source of black and burst, often with additional facilities such as test signal generation. Many installations make use of a test signal generator for this purpose as the freedom to reconfigure sources is not compromised by one of them being tied to sourcing genlock video.

The simplified studio, as depicted in Figure 8.1, shows how the mixing point is the timing reference for all studio input sources, the actual measurements being made at the mixer output. Referring back to Figure 4.15 for a moment will show how two sources may appear with a timing difference. To allow alteration and addition to the system, a jackfield intercept panel can be introduced. This offers quick and convenient source interchanging but in so doing, the jackfield becomes a timed point in itself,

Returning to timing. We have so far made no mention of colour and it is now opportune to distinguish between component and composite studio design. With component working, the timing requirement is similar to that already described and conforms to what is called monochrome timing. The term 'monochrome' correctly describes 'one-colour', which is not black and white, or pictures without colour. Monochrome is strictly any colour, but one only, which therefore still constitutes a colour signal. But strictly correct terms become abused and where monochrome timing is stated it implies black and white or luminance timing. Timing requirements for component video are based on an accuracy of 0.1 μs.

Component video demands accurate matching of the three circuits. Colour registration, that is the overlaying of the colour difference signals, must be done accurately if colour fringing is to be avoided. Registration of the colour and luminance signals is less demanding. If care is taken over design and installation, these requirements should not cause difficulties, and, once in place, measurement on any regular basis should not be necessary. An example of a component WFM is shown in Figure 8.3.

The importance of test signals must never be overlooked. Any installation worthy of the name 'studio' will include colour bars as a source to the mixer.

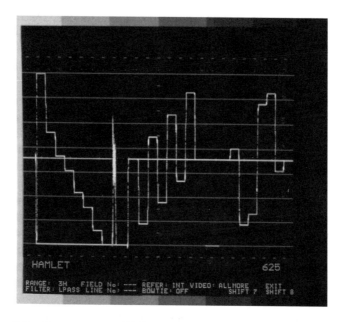

Figure 8.3 Component WFM. Colour bars displayed in parade— luminance followed by blue and red colour difference signals. These are 75% colour bars and so the red and blue signals therefore appear at the lower amplitude. Operationally, it is more usual to view only the lumi-nance waveform as the overall level has greater significance than colour alone.

To be able to 'cut'—or output—colour bars to the destination is good video practice. In doing so a known test signal has been subject to mixer processing, and one can have confidence that any changes that result will be immediately apparent.

Consider this ...

We sometimes see colour fringing in newsprint. The colours—cyan, magenta, yellow, with black added for tonal rendition—may not always register. Colour fringing is a term that might describe the effect of mistimed component signals. How might a delay of the Cb signal over the others be seen? Would it be horizontal or vertical? In fact, could it be both? A clue: think microseconds and lines.

Composite colour timing

Although component operation has overtaken composite as the principle production method, many smaller operators remain composite based, or have elements of composite video to contend with. Nor will it do harm to reiterate the complexity of PAL and NTSC for these standards have had too great an influence to be put to one side just yet. And it must be said, a great deal of what follows will be found applicable in some way or other to component video operation.

By far the most stringent parameter of composite is time. The timing requirement when colour TV was first propounded, was considered then to stretch the available technology to its limits. Programme operations had already begun to expand beyond the confines of four studio walls. The demand to use external, or remote, picture sources as well brought about timing techniques so elaborate as to verge on the mystic. But it was done, new production standards were set and are now the norm.

We have seen from Chapter 5 how the whole colour spectrum is contained in one rotation of the vector of chrominance subcarrier. A metre of cable causes about 5 ns of delay or about 8° of vector phase shift. Bear in mind these are rationalised values for the subcarrier frequencies of both TV standards.

Try this ...

If you have a vectorscope, conduct a simple test. Measure the phase delay of a length of cable by using a vectorscope. Figure 8.4 shows you what to do.

Mixer timing procedure

The video mixer is a comprehensive control for picture cutting, mixing, fading and montaging (building an image from various separate picture elements. The film term 'compositing' is avoided here because of confusion with composite video. The video term is 'mixer effects' or 'mixeffects', or simply 'ME'). Where mixer effects are used to key, inlay, mix or fade, more than one video source contributes elements of the signal. All these must be in perfect synchronism for luminance and chrominance. Luminance timing, or line sync timing, is termed variously as 'H timing', or 'H phase', sometimes simply 'line timing'. Composite chrominance timing is termed 'C phase', 'colour phase,' 'φ phase', 'CSC phase', or 'SC phase'. These are the usual terms applied to the timing controls referred to in Figure 8.2.

And again, we use the example of composite video because it will cover the subject more fully. Where reference is made specifically to features of PAL or NTSC, it is not necessarily saying to the component worker 'turn off'. It may, in the end, point the way to a deeper understanding.

Control of line timing and colour phase are independent of each other, a further indicator that even in one-circuit composite video, luminance and chrominance still remain discrete signals.

Where only one source is selected on the mixer, the whole of the signal will be passed, including the sync and burst. Where a picture is made from more than one source, the mixer must decide which sync and burst to use. It cannot pass both for reasons already described. How it chooses will depend on its design. It could insert black and burst. Black is a production requirement, as in a fade-to-black; the mixer output will then be simply black and burst. A source of black and burst may be derived from the genlock distribution. In many cases the mixer will itself produce black and burst for source genlock and for its own internal consumption. 'Black' for the composite system is inclusive of colour burst. In component form it is only the sync pulse stream.

Yet another picture source provided by the mixer is 'infill'. Caption cutouts may be infilled with a colour, or matte. Any other coloured mixer effect will also use internally generated mattes.

Now the mixer is becoming a signal source in its own right with its own black and matte generators. All are subject to the same requirements of synchronism as any other mixer input. These features are specific to individual designs; how they are dealt with will be evident from the manuals describing them. The basic principle of timing must remain intact, however, regardless of where the picture, or parts thereof, come from.

To carry out a timing check, start by choosing a reliable known source as a reference against which to compare. One would be forgiven for suggesting colour bars. Understandably so, but beware! Colour bars is primarily a test signal of level, luminance and colour, and may not have good enough time accuracy. In most cases it will, and where a comprehensive test signal generator is part of the genlock, or SPG, system, it can be relied upon. Check beforehand.

There's another source, and by design, a very reliable one. The hidden source of black—the sync bed that the mixer must have always available to it. Black—in whatever form we require—may also be available from the test signal generator. This is the ideal timing reference, for all picture sources will at some time have their syncs stripped away to be replaced with mixer black. If you wonder about this, check out the mixer handbook.

Or you may choose a camera if your mixer is a more basic design that does not have its own black generator. In these designs this one source, sometimes called 'master video', will supply the syncs under the various special effects activities of the mixer.

Whichever way is decided upon, refer to the handbook for guidance. Mixers are complex and need the same care and understanding as cameras.

For our purposes we will take a camera as our master timing source. Let us assume that the chosen one has a camera control unit. Control units detach the actual picture sources from the mixer; they act as interfaces and one advantage is to make the timing process simpler—we deal with the control unit, not the camera. The distinction is important.

Which camera is often decided for us. The one most often used, or the most stable, may be the best of a disparate bunch ... You may choose a quite different source: graphics or captions. Avoid roaming sources, those available to other areas by routeing systems or physical movement. If none of the sources is fixed, the choice is open but go for the one which seems the best, the most modern, or even the simplest. It's an open question so take advice and use your judgement.

And we are going to be thorough ... so select the camera on the mixer so all the slight variations introduced by the mixer are revealed. Mixers can have a multiplicity of paths for the various effects they create, but we want the main, or programme output, usually designated PGM. This is the simplest path, and by depressing the button for that source it is routed directly to the output.

Adjust WFM and vectorscope to place the camera display correctly against the graticules, bearing in mind that it is H timing on the WFM, with C phase on the vectorscope for composite. When this is done, cut up all the other cameras in turn, watching their relative timings of line sync leading edges and phase changes of colour burst. Note there is no mention of colour bars on the cameras. It really doesn't matter whether pictures or bars is present on camera outputs (or any other source) as synchronisation only concerns line sync and colour burst. We are now dealing with the part of video that is outside the picture period. Timing is black and burst and nothing else—at least for the present.

Having said that, it's not easy for an engineer worth his or her salt to ignore the picture, so switch on colour bars and see how they compare as you cut through the sources one by one. Differences will be due to individual

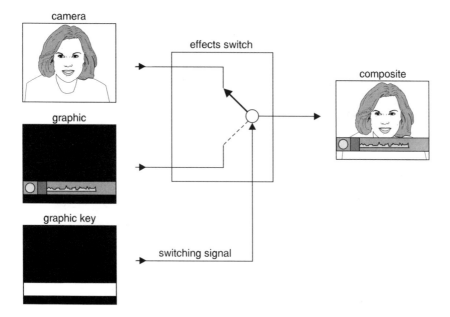

Figure 8.7   Timing an inserted graphic. The camera has inserted into it a graphic. The resulting mix-effects signal has the camera's sync and burst. Therefore, when checking at mixer out, timing and colour phase errors (which apply to the graphic) will not be seen on WFM or vectorscope. They will, however, be evident on picture. Adjust H and C by monitoring at mixer inputs first camera then graphic. Check with picture.

change over sync pulses and colour burst. H and C timing must be correct if the graphic is to be correctly positioned and true to colour.

Figure 8.7 presents a potential problem when viewing at the mixer out. Here we will see only one sync and burst: that from one or other of the sources—the camera in this case. The output will appear timed and in phase, and looking perfectly normal. The graphic though, may appear on picture shifted right or left, and if composite video, with changed colour. Selecting the sources independently to the test set at the mixer inputs, as in Figure 8.2 and seen in Figure 8.6, will show the errors.

The picture will reveal a lot in this case. The eye will easily spot colour and saturation differences when checking between the two sources separately and then the final. Timing can, at this stage, be carried out using the picture but check what the test set is telling you whilst doing so.

How much easier in component, we all say. Yet we must not forget that the two inputs in Figure 8.7 each have three components. Six circuits to be timed. For this very reason, composite held the ascendancy for so long against three-circuit component. We will see later a specialised method of checking that all three components arrive at the same time.

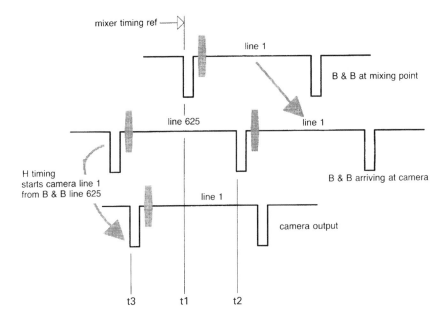

mixer timing ref

line 1

B & B at mixing point

line 625

line 1

H timing
starts camera line 1
from B & B line 625

B & B arriving at camera

line 1

camera output

t3   t1   t2

Figure 8.8   Remote camera timing. To synchronise the remote camera picture with other sources, it must start its scan early. Looking at Line 1, the black and burst genlock signal is delayed from t1 to t2 over the distance to the camera. Adjusting camera H timing to compensate demands that camera Line 1 *is started earlier* than Line 1 of genlock. To do this the camera generator refers to Line 625 of the previous field, starting camera Line 1 at t3.

Installing a remote camera

This is as much an exercise in the ramifications of timing but it has practical relevance as well. A remote camera without local control unit will require its own feed of genlock extended out to it, presenting a potential difficulty. To get its signal back in sync with local cameras means that it must be advanced in time. Figure 8.8 describes the process, and the principle behind advanced genlock. Or how a camera is able to start its scan by referring to an earlier part of the waveform. Composite colour phase is dealt with in the same way.

No mention has been made so far about frame and field timing. That is because it is only necessary to identify a line number; everything will fall into place from that. The genlock system compares waveforms at the field sync and identifies which field is which.

But there is more to the video system than this, as will be seen when we consider the mechanics of video tape recording. In the meantime, let's look at pictures.

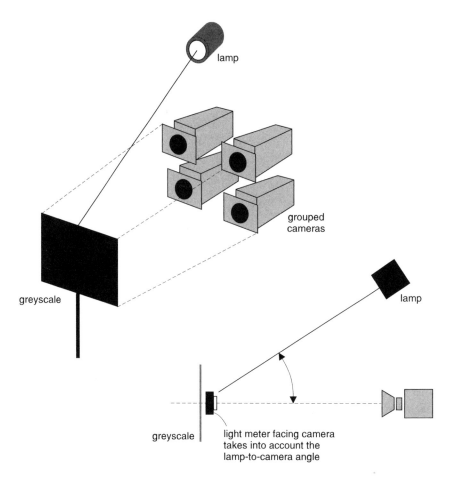

greyscale

lamp

grouped
cameras

lamp

greyscale | light meter facing camera
takes into account the
lamp-to-camera angle

Figure 8.10   Cameras pointing at a greyscale. The cameras are tightly grouped and the greyscale is at right angles to the cameras. The lamp is at an angle such that reflections from the surface of the greyscale are not seen by any camera. The greyscale is evenly lit. When measuring the light level at the greyscale, always face the meter to the cameras, not the lamp; that way you measure what the cameras see.

If possible avoid higher settings in the interests of lamp life. Light level should be similar to that on set and should be adjusted by altering the lamp to greyscale distance, or by changing the light intensity by spotting or flooding the lamp.

Camera control

In a multicamera studio, camera control is carried out from the control room. The camera operator has the usual control of camera position, lens angle and focus, whilst pedestal, iris, and colour are controlled remotely from the operational or production area. In cases where no camera operator is employed, there will be the additional controls for camera movements; tracking, pan and tilt, lens angle and focus. Sometimes a dedicated room is set aside for vision control and lighting.

The remote camera control panel will have the following picture controls as part of the operational control panels, or OCPs:

- lens iris to control exposure;
- pedestal to set the picture blacks.

These are mechanically part of the same control; a quadrant throttle-like lever is the iris. The rotary head of the lever is the pedestal, often referred to as 'black' or 'lift' in studio.

- colour gain: control of red and blue camera gains;
- colour black: red and blue pedestal.

There may be gamma, overall gain to set the sensitivity, dynamic contrast control, and other facilities as well. But the main ones, as described above, are the basic controls to set up and match all the cameras accurately.

Firstly cap the cameras, that is iris all the lenses to close. Now pedestals can be checked—whether or not the nominal 3% is used is by the way—the object is to make all cameras the same. Use the picture monitor and the waveform and pay particular attention to relating the two. The picture will, at present, be black, but will reveal more about the cameras as each is selected in turn. Look for any slight colour variation in black, by operating pedestal and colour blacks differences can be minimised. The object is to aim for perfection but with emphasis on getting them all the same, perfection may have to be compromised a little.

Choose one camera as master and adjust colour blacks until true black is achieved. Use the WFM and work to minimise subcarrier if monitoring composite. If component, aim to minimise Cr and Cb displays on the WFM. Use a vectorscope if available, adjusting the colour blacks to centre the display. This applies to component vectors as well.

The picture monitor will obviously need to be set-up properly, but briefly switching the monitor to monochrome will show the slightest greyscale errors. Monitor set-up is dealt with in the Appendix.

Having satisfied yourself that the cameras all produce similar blacks, open the lenses. Expose to bring the white patches to 100%. Note at what level the whites of both greyscale wedges reach; it is almost certain that they will not be the same. Slight variations of light level will cause a few per cent error, but this is not a serious problem as long as the same white patch is used for measurement of all the cameras. Be sure to avoid getting confused by over exposing into the white clip point. It will be quite obvious when this

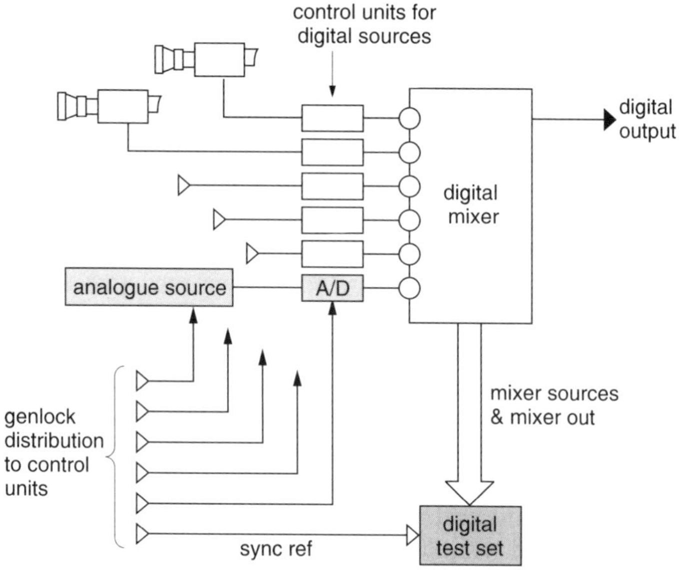

Figure 8.11   A typical digital studio. The digital sources have genlock in the usual way. The single analogue source has genlock applied to both itself and its analogue to digital converter. It need not be closely timed... the digital mixer with synchronised inputs will take up any remaining difference.

Digital timing

The 'sync pulse' as we have come to know it, doesn't exist in digital video. It is replaced by timing reference signals (TRS), and there are two per line; short binary word groups, one marking the start of picture the other marking the end. On converting back to analogue, the original syncs are regenerated.

It's an irony but the genlock source is often black and burst—using existing facilities wherever possible saves cost—modern test signal generation and SPGs are no exception. It is only sync timing that's used, the colour burst is of course, ignored.

Where a component requires a timing accuracy of 100 ns (0.1 µs), a digital mixer has its own means to time its sources. The tolerance may be half a line, which is 30 or so microseconds, which is a very wide acceptance indeed. In a studio complex it is most unlikely that 30 µs difference between source timing would occur, but clocks have still to run at the same speed, and genlock does that. Yet that need for close timing, which so greatly influenced analogue studio design, has now largely disappeared.

Composite video can still appear in the most up-to-date digital installations. Large monitor stacks are often cost-cut to make use of existing analogue designs. These require analogue feeds and composite has a continuing role here, often in YC form—separate luminance and chrominance, but still based on PAL or NTSC and perfectly adequate for the job.

The home viewer too—we should not forget that most homes continue to view analogue composite—is not to be forgotten in this age of advancement. Composite has shortcomings and we must remain mindful of its artefacts. A typical TV set is ideal to check for this. Use the off-air receiver . . . provide it with a video feed of studio out as well as an aerial.

If all this seems very new and rather daunting . . .

You will need two invaluable resources: time and a picture-eye. The former is a management matter. The latter is about you and you alone. If you have an eye for a picture it leaves only the question of time. It will take time to 'learn the picture'. We talk of 'black', 'white', and 'no-colour'. Experienced practitioners take these things in their stride. Experience and practice. Play with cameras. Experiment. Above all think and be disciplined. Relate what you see to what you do. Invest in time, time and more time.

However, while analogue will give some sign of pending failure by loss of picture quality, digital will not. Some prediction is obviously advisable in the digital system, and one example is mentioned later in Chapter 11.

Setting up to edit

In Figure 9.2 we see a basic edit system. Assume a component analogue system—composite is now obsolete in professional video tape editing. As with the studio, much of what is said here will apply to a digital system. Let us begin with the recording, or edit machine, and make a test recording of colour bars. The source of these should be a local generator and checked to make sure they are good. Before recording check that the machine is in the correct mode, check with the manual about the TBC and record settings. These will be subject to an engineering procedure that will optimise them. There may be specific control positions referred to in the manual and these should be adhered to. Record about half a minute, or more, of colour bars.

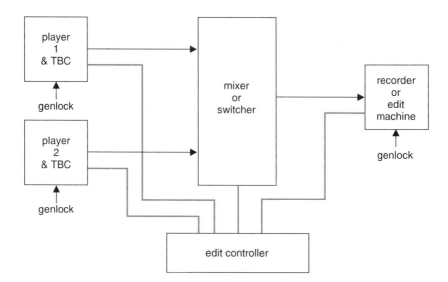

Figure 9.2   Basic edit system. The mixer may be the same design as that used in the studio. Timebase correction is incorporated into each machine, making them appear as standard sources with timing adjustments. There may also be framing adjustment. For editing, the mixer is under the control of the edit controller with the whole operation controlled by **timecode**. Timecode allocates a number to every picture frame on the video tapes. The edit controller uses timecode to know tape positions and to control playing, recording and spooling and also the mixer effects for mixing and compositing.

It may be questioned as to why it is so important to set up the replay side of the record machine. The edit monitoring is from this machine and the programme can only be accessed through the replay side.

Play back and check the result. Adjust the playback controls until the replayed colour bars are correct. The controls are:

1 **Gain:** sets overall signal level or amplitude. There may be a separate control for sync amplitude.
2 **Lift:** this is pedestal or black level.
3 **Saturation:** the amplitude of chrominance.

Playback could appear distorted. Recorded colour bars won't look quite like those recorded. With composite monitoring the subcarrier envelope could show distortion, and will point to the more severe treatment of the colour signals by the recording process. Set the gain control (Y level) to make the white bar 100%. Adjust lift (pedestal or black) so that the black bar is at 0%. Make sure it's not below, it can only be set properly by raising, then carefully setting back to black level. Do not, at least at this stage, put in any pedestal unless it is part of your standard operation. Finally, saturation (sometimes referred to as 'colour'). Adjust to make Cr and Cb fill the component WFM graticule. When using composite monitoring make the lowest edge of the green bar envelope coincident with black level at 0% (obviously lift must be set beforehand).

It is good practice to go through the procedure a second time... it takes only a moment. Recording degradation makes precise adjustment less easy and repeating it is never wasted.

When everything is satisfactory, 'stripe' or 'black' the edit tape. The edit tape takes the edited programme and black and burst is recorded on the whole length of an unused tape. In the process, timecode must also be recorded so that the edit controller can recognise the tape position and can therefore control the edit machine.

All recorded programmes should have colour bars on the first 30 seconds of tape, which will be used to set up subsequent replay machines. It is always assumed when accepting recorded material that the colour bars preceding the programme are correct, hence the care attached to recording them in the first place.

On the play-in side—the source machines—signal levels may be unknown and unpredictable. Line-up should be carried out whenever a tape is changed. This is imperative as recorded source material may differ, tape performance varies, the recorder itself may change. Recordings are outside the control of the edit system; they could be sourced from anywhere and on any equipment, leading to considerable variation in all parameters.

Also, where the source recording is a camera, bear in mind the signal levels of actual pictures. In the two previous chapters we looked at how cameras may produce signals exceeding 100%. The camera colour bars are

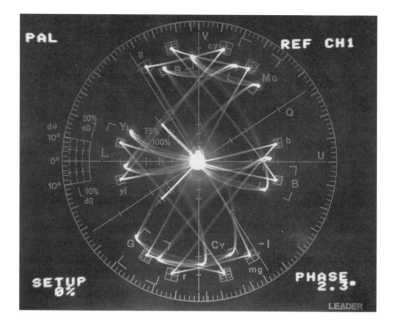

Figure 9.4   Horizontal wipe showing phase error. Vectors of the split screen shown in Figure 9.3. Both sets of colour bars will appear because the vectorscope displays the frame divided between the colour bars from both sources. Source 1 is correctly phased while source 2 leads by 10°, and is also low saturation. Only one burst is present; that associated with source 1. Component vectors will be similar but without colour burst.

If the source tapes are swapped it will be necessary to go through all these checks again.

The more the procedure is gone through, the quicker it will become; a forgotten or sloppy line-up is an embarrassing waste of editing and production time. Be methodical and develop an operational discipline. Experience is so valuable here: knowing waveforms and the equipment, what it can do and what it will not.

We may feel that component is a blessing: indeed it is where tape degradation and timing is concerned, but there are three signals that must match perfectly. Keep an eye on the picture for colour changes: they may be subtle, but could point to internal machine line-up. It is unlikely that the measurement test set will indicate the small errors that will be evident on picture. Composite monitoring has some advantages—to the experienced user it can indicate faults or errors very quickly—but it is important to ensure that it is accurate and its own line-up checked out regularly.

One final parameter of the composite age remains: SC-H phase. It is mentioned here because there is a parallelism with editing MPEG digital video.

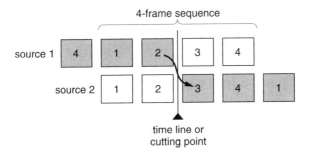

Figure 9.5 Framing around the cutting point. Aligning the 4-frame sequence on a time-line, showing a cut switching from source 1 to source 2. The sources must be aligned by frame number: 1 to 1, 2 to 2, and so on. Although the cutting point is free to move anywhere along the sequence, a 4-frame alignment is restrictive where scene action requires fine adjustment of one shot against the other. NTSC is less so with its 2-frame sequence.

The Appendix has the technical background to SC-H phase. In short, NTSC and PAL do not possess adjacent frames which are similar. Of course, the picture content may differ—but we are here talking about the pulse sequence that lies beneath. In NTSC it repeats only every two frames, in PAL it's every four.

Figure 9.5 shows how a long frame sequence restricts the editor because of the rigid alignment of the source material. Chapter 6 concluded with compression and the MPEG sequence, and the constraints this placed on the editor.

Examples of digital tape standards

Sony Digital Betacam has taken over from Betacam SP as one of the principal broadcast acquisition mediums. It is a 4:2:2 system with a 2:1 compression ratio which may be regarded as almost loss-less, i.e. in practice very little material is discarded by the compression process.

DVCPRO is 4:1:1 with a 5:1 compression ratio and is aimed at low-end broadcast and news.

DVCAM uses 4:2:0, a colour standard which provides better balance of vertical to horizontal resolution, and is aimed at corporate/professional users, and utilises similar compression. In reality, any of these systems might be found working in the television and video industry. Each has advantages and disadvantages, not least that of wide variation in physical size and price.

it may have signal demands made of it that are beyond its capabilities. The list can go on.

Linearity and phase distortion

Tonal compression, or non-linear distortion, is a common example. A camera's dynamic contrast control can be described as a designed distortion. It does not become a fault unless its operation falls outside its specification, or outside the picture requirements. It is important to recognise what is a fault and what is not. We will use the literal definition of the word; for our purposes distortion is a fault condition.

Non-linear distortion can arise in a number of situations. Equipment performance deteriorates as ageing components cause the circuitry parameters to change. Considerable effort is taken to ensure circuitry design has sufficient tolerance to combat this but there comes a point when the design is no longer able to cope. The simple ramp signal is able to reveal this, as Figure 10.1 shows. Colour bars will also show the effect but less obviously, as Figure 10.2 reveals.

Another clue to the presence of non-linear distortion is where sync to picture ratio departs from the 70/30 ratio (NTSC uses a slightly different

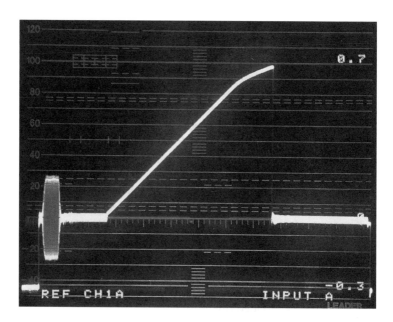

Figure 10.1 Non-linear distortion. A ramp signal is a straight line, but here it has become curved by circuit non-linearity. The higher tones—those approaching white—will be compressed. Compare to the camera contrast control described in Chapter 7.

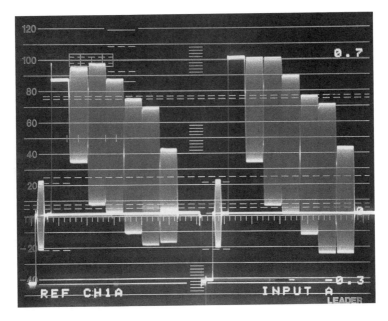

Figure 10.2 Colour bars and non-linear distortion. This is a parade display of faulty signal on the left and original on the right. Note how the white bar does not reach 100%. Distortion of the chrominance envelope indicates that something is amiss but not exactly what.

ratio: see Appendix). When the test signal is replaced by a picture, watch out for the clip level of peak white, check that it is 0.7 V and that syncs are 0.3 V. If one is right and the other not, there's obviously an error somewhere but you won't know whether it's incorrect clip level or non-linear distortion until you run a test. Non-linear distortion could have occurred after camera peak white clippers have done their job.

An example is a distribution amplifier. The device should be transparent allowing the signal to pass through without change. The waveform occupies so much space, it has an amplitude that must fit into the circuitry parameters: power supplies must provide the necessary power. When ageing takes place, circuitry components drift out of tolerance and signal headroom reduces or shifts. It is the signal extremes, syncs or white, that suffer as a result.

A variation of non-linear distortion produces another common fault in composite video. Differential phase distortion often arises from the same conditions that cause non-linear distortion. Yellow has a high luminance value and occupies one extreme of the waveform; it is the first colour to suffer this kind of distortion. Figure 10.2 shows the yellow envelope is no longer symmetrical about its mean luminance value. Figure 10.3 is the vectorscope's view of what has happened and reveals something else: the fault has caused the yellow bar to be shortened and skewed indicating that both saturation and phase errors are present.

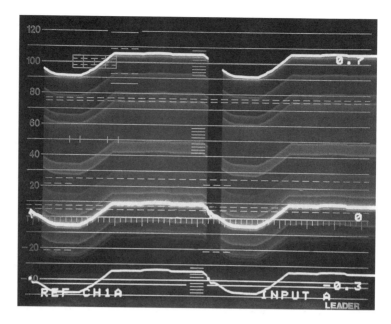

Figure 10.5   Power interference. The time scale is 40 ms. This is the picture frame rate of two fields (2 V) and the interfering waveform of the 50 Hz power line is therefore a similar rate.

test sets will do this. It may however be an imperfect correction in extreme cases. The best solution is to understand why and deal with the cause: keep signal and power circuits well separated.

Frequency distortion

From earlier chapters on signal transmission, we saw how a signal's bandwidth was worked out. In Figure 10.6 the colour bars have low chrominance due to high-frequency loss in a circuit, possibly that resulting from a long length of cable. This will give pictures of reduced colour saturation.

High-frequency loss and edge response are closely linked. Bandwidth controls the signal transition rate from black to white and vice versa. Edge response, or rise time, as the term is called, describes this. Standard video has a lower limit of 25 Hz frame rate and an upper limit of 5.5 MHz, which is the video bandwidth. These are the limits described as the 'half power points'—where the signal transmission falls to half power due to circuit losses. High-frequency (HF) loss takes place in all circuits, with cable and amplifiers all contributing towards the condition. Other effects also manifest themselves from HF loss. Slowing of edge response shows up in line sync and the rise time becomes longer as in Figure 10.7. The design intention is for the HF limit to be just high enough for the signal to pass without loss. Excessive bandwidth is wasteful.

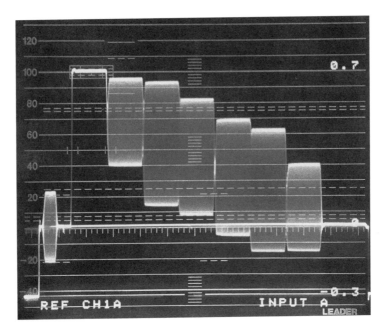

Figure 10.6 High-frequency loss. The colour bars show low saturation because of a condition in the circuit causing high-frequency loss. Colour subcarrier lies at the upper end of the band and is therefore most affected. Compare this to the colour bars in Figure 5.6.

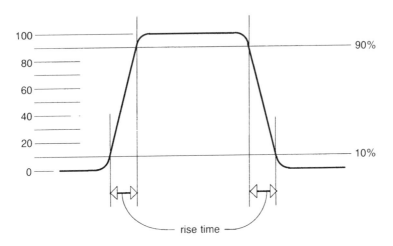

Figure 10.7 How rise time is measured. This is a pulse of signal from black level to white. Rise time is measured between 10% and 90% levels, either in the rising or falling transitions. Note that the waveform shown has rounded corners as well. The shape is that produced by a practical circuit having normal bandwidth limitation. The rise time must be sufficient for the signal concerned.

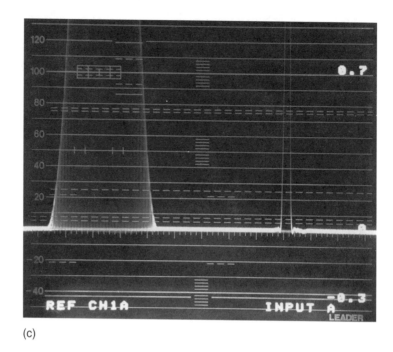

(c)

Figure 10.8c   (continued) The pulse and bar. (c) Magnified portions of chroma and 1T pulses.

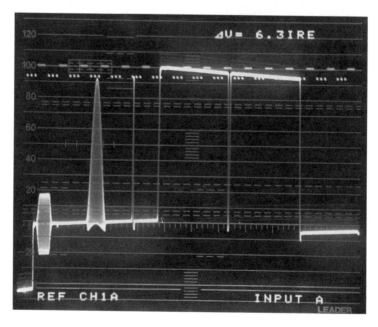

Figure 10.9   The bar measures LF loss. How much sag the bar has indicates LF loss. The cursors show this in percentage (shown in IRE values).

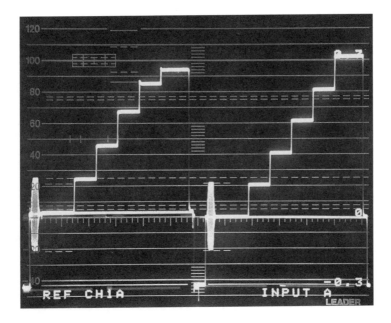

Figure 10.10   The step. The step for non-linearity measurement. The equal step heights will vary if non-linearity is present. Compare with the ramp test signal used in previous tests.

part of the signal were to be distorted. In each case the signal must enter the system as perfectly as possible and must not cause parameters to alter by any variation in the synchronising components of the signal. Three more examples are described in Figures 10.10, 10.11 and 10.12.

Figure 10.13 is an example of how component monitoring may reveal a typical fault.

Calibration

All test signals are calibrated signals, and colour bars are the universal calibrated test signal, by definition. WFMs and vectorscopes have calibration checks. These are internal signals used to check the accuracy of the equipment, a kind of self-check. Calibrated cursors, on the other hand, are adjustable markers that are placed against the signal, giving the value as a read-out. Such an example is shown in Figure 10.9, where the sag of the bar is measured by the cursor positions.

Comparing signal to signal

So far we have measured signals by comparing them to a scale or calibrated waveform. An alternative is to compare like with like; that is, to a chosen

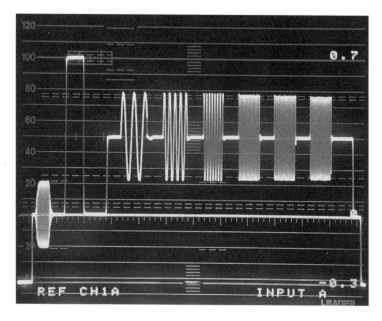

Figure 10.11   Multiburst. Multiburst is a group of frequency bursts. As the signal passes through a circuit, the bursts' amplitudes will alter if frequency distortion is present.

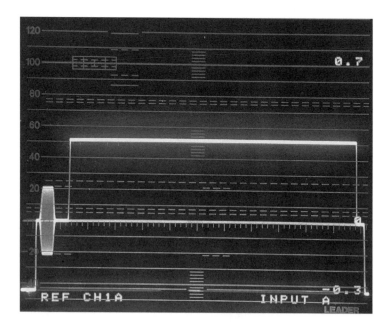

Figure 10.12   Flat field. Flat field is a uniform level over the complete line and field. Shown here as 100% flat field, it is used to determine the low-frequency performance of a circuit. The flatness of the signal should remain constant from the top of the field to the bottom. It may also be used to check picture display for uniformity of grey.

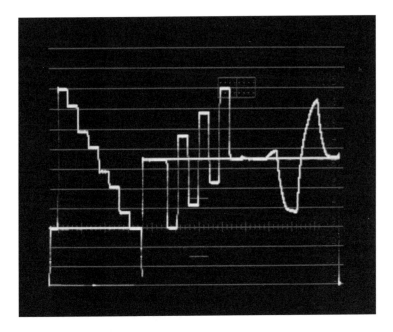

Figure 10.13 A faulty component signal. This signal shows a fault condition. The Cr component is very distorted, showing serious high-frequency loss, which probably results from a damaged cable or connector. Compare with Figure 6.1. Why is this obviously an analogue fault and not a digital one? How might the fault manifest itself on picture?

signal, which is adjusted to be exactly that required for a specific operation. The important point here is that the chosen signal is now a standard, or master. Any source may be used; it may be a graphic or a camera, whichever is convenient and reliable. It is connected to a two-input WFM and set up precisely. The other sources are connected to the other WFM input in turn, and by switching between the two, any differences to the master source will immediately show.

Alternatively, if the WFM offers the facility, overlay the two signals. Switch speeds as fast as line rate will produce a 'parade', each successive line shown by the WFM will be the next source, and so on, one after the other. The YCrCb component waveform is a parade signal—we all know the three components are synchronous, yet they appear on the display one after the other, as in Figure 10.13.

Figure 10.14 shows another method.

Comparing signal to signal is primarily to get matched signals. As a measurement method it is quick and accurate but does require that the master is exact. On the other hand, any specific features of your system can be replicated by setting up the master as you require. In setting up cameras in the studio the final trimming of black, exposure and colour is done on a picture monitor.

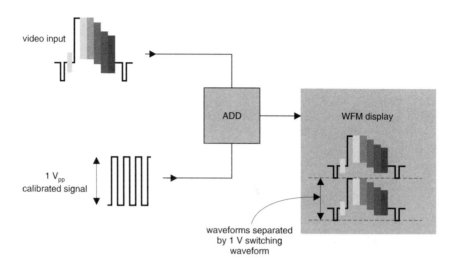

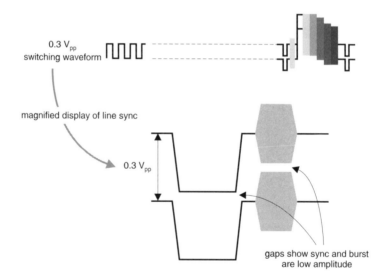

Figure 10.14   Calibrated switching waveform. The calibrated waveform is a square wave of higher frequency than line rate. When added to the video input, it results in the displays shown. The waveform appears twice, displaced vertically by the calibration voltage. The magnified example shows the line sync and burst are not 0.3 V.

The subject of test equipment is extensive and only a brief insight can be given here. Test equipment manufacturers' literature is always useful, often giving valuable advice and background information to video measurement.

CHAPTER 11

DIGITAL SPECIALITIES

While this chapter is titled 'digital' some of the procedures described here may equally be applicable to analogue. As with Chapter 10, these examples of test and measurement are in no way intended to be definitive. There are others, either already in existence or likely to appear in the future.

Bowtie and lightning

Bowtie (see Figure 11.1) checks for equality of level and timing between component circuits. Lightning serves a similar function but uses a vectoral display of Y against Cb and Cr, and like bowtie it is a specialised test designed to give a quick appraisal of circuit conditions. But, whereas bowtie requires its own test signal to be sent, lightning makes use of colour bars.

Checking gamut with arrowhead

Gamut is the colour range that is usable by or acceptable to, a colour display. A distinction should be drawn between gamut and illegal colours. 100% colour bars were—and still are in some instances—considered outside the video standard for transmission, and therefore illegal. Gamut, however, will vary depending on the type of display. In television the display is based on the standard TV receiver, which is CRT based. Other kinds of display should have similar characteristics to the CRT to conform to the standard. Gamut becomes a problem due to a number of issues. Colours may be synthesised as in a graphics suite, and despite the controls applied by the standard, it is still possible to create colours outside the video gamut. Also, there is the potential for modification to colour in digital effects. Component colour itself is an unnatural concept as no colour can exist as hue alone, there is always an element of luminance present. Cr and Cb may very easily be changed to make them reproduce outside gamut, and in some instances, to become illegal.

A very real practical problem arises with the displayed picture. Not all react to out-of-gamut colours in the same way, and it is not unknown

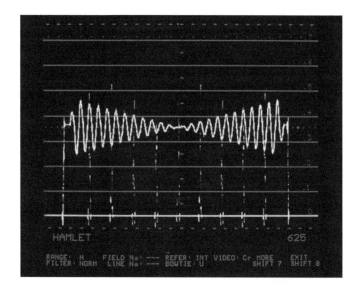

Figure 11.1   Bowtie and component circuit discrepancies. Bowtie uses a fixed frequency sine wave feeding all three component circuits. That feeding Y differs slightly in frequency from that for Cr and Cb. At the destination Y is subtracted from Cr and Cb giving the characteristic bowtie shape (the example shown here is Cr). Where a discrepancy exists between either of the colour circuits and Y the display will be distorted. A timing error will shift the 'squeeze' of the bow away from the centre. A level error causes the 'squeeze' to thicken.

for pictures, side by side, to show different colours. Gamut warning has therefore become relevant to digital video.

Tests, such as 'arrowhead' and 'diamond', make use of RGB displayed in such a way that values which exceed the gamut are easily seen. Figure 11.2 shows arrowhead.

Two examples of tests which apply to the more engineering aspects of video transmission are included here because they often appear on test gear, and may therefore provoke interest. They also serve as pointers to the direction digital test and measurement is taking: simple, reliable, but specific to certain checks.

Eye display—the circuit tester

Digital circuits operate at much higher frequencies and are therefore more susceptible to flaws, damage or misuse. The one redeeming factor is, of course, the tolerant nature of the digital signal. Figure 11.3 shows an idealised example of a digital data stream and how it might appear at its destination. Eye display is a good example of an easy to use technique that provides a reliable answer to one specific problem; signal quality at the destination.

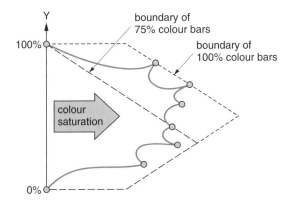

Figure 11.2 Gamut check with arrowhead. The area delineated by the arrowhead defines the gamut limits. Signals complying with the 75% limit must lie on or within the 75% boundary. The 100% boundary is the outer one. The signal shown is of 100% colour bars, white and black lie along the vertical Y axis, the six coloured bars appear in order round the diagram. Colours appearing outside the arrowhead are out of gamut.

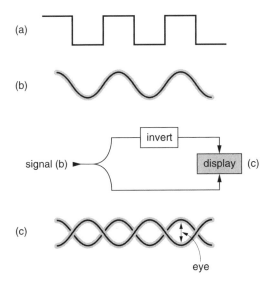

Figure 11.3 Eye display checking the received signal. (a) The digital signal in idealised form; a series of 0s and 1s, perfectly shaped and square. (b) After arrival at the destination, the edges are rounded and the circuit has collected a great deal of noise en route. The received signal (b) has successive 0s and 1s overlaid, the result of which is displayed in (c). (c) The clear space between the two is the 'eye height'. As the received signal worsens the eye closes, the more open the better the signal quality.

EDH and CRC

Error Detection and Handing (EDH) and Cyclic Redundancy Check (CRC) are to do with digital video's auto-checking system. The principle is to detect data errors in each digital video field and to report a qualitative value. This is called 'errored second', a figure based on number of fields in error in a given time. CRC is the technique of checking at successive stages and passing the information forward so that subsequent checks reveal the whole circuit performance from start to finish. The checks are of a 'go/no-go', type, where an error arises it is flagged by an indicator.

A check at the source, EDA (Error Detected Already), will determine if an error has occurred before the signal enters the chain, either transmission, recording or whatever. Further errors along the route will reveal at the destination the quality of the whole chain. Where an error is spotted an EDH (Error Detected Here) is flagged. Therefore, if EDA and EDH are clear, there have been no detected errors.

Note the abbreviation confusion of the term 'EDH'—'H' may mean either 'handling' or 'here'. In most cases it will be taken as the former—the generic term. In fact many systems do no support checking at source so the confusion will not always arise.

Errors are caused by noise corrupting the digital signal, either as isolated incidents, or more extended ones. Cable length has a great influence over error rate, the longer the cable the worse it gets, not forgetting its condition and that of its connectors. Errors can also occur during recording and replay, signal switching and any form of processing.

Other flags check within equipment. IDH (Internal error Detected Here) and IDA (Internal error Detected Already) point to specific processing units with self-checking procedures reporting errors.

One would think that here is the ideal answer to a long-standing problem but unfortunately EDH is not supported by all the sections of the video chain; some video mixers do not pass these valuable little indicators of signal state, but it is expected that as new developments take place such shortcomings will be overcome.

Digital video has given rise to the development of a range of test signals aimed at engineering and maintenance. It has to be accepted that much of the technical side is very specialised, whereas this book is aimed at the newcomer. It is therefore unwise to carry out adjustments without a full understanding of what you do. Take advice is the advice constantly repeated.

Portable instrumentation

Microelectronics continue to offer more facilities with greater reliability. The essential requirement though, never varies. Accuracy and reliability—there is little point in using a ruler with 'wrong inches'. The technology now makes possible a whole range of reliable and portable instruments performing a variety of tasks at affordable prices.

In deciding how to equip a new (or existing) facility, one good base system and a series of smaller simpler ones for use in the field, make sense. Give plenty of thought to your needs, choose carefully and buy wisely, but be prepared to update as systems and techniques change. Choose a component/composite WFM with vector display, plus a portable kit if you do location work. And don't forget the picture!

CHAPTER 12

USING THE PICTURE

Setting up the picture

There is no greater confusion in video operations than that caused by incorrect monitor set-up. Different monitors will show different pictures and where monitors are working side by side it is particularly irritating when they do not match each other. Avoid mixing products by different manufacturers wherever possible. Monitor set-up is a critical operation requiring a known signal source, and should ideally be carried out by one person following exactly the same procedure.

PLUGE

The most common picture display set-up is PLUGE (picture line-up and generating equipment), which has a step waveform with additional 5% steps above and below video black level: see Figure 12.1. The four-step contrast set-up may be measured and compared to the picture display manufacturer's specification. It may also be used to compare monitor-to-monitor contrast and gamma—not by eye, not even the most experienced eye is truly reliable, but using a proprietary procedure. Setting brightness is critical to 1%, but this can be done by eye. Brightness is adjusted until the darker of the two 5% bars is just visible. Alternatively, setting the lighter of the 5% bars to be just visible gives a lower brightness setting, and is appropriate when working with a fixed pedestal or NTSC set-up.

Vical

Vical picture set-up is designed for location camera use, and is part of the Vical measurement system: see Figure 12.2. The test signal is inserted into the source picture and therefore appears to the picture display as integral with that source. A capped camera with pedestal set to 3%, will show slightly brighter than the black bar which is at video black of 0%. Brightness may be set to just perceive this difference. The technique is very adaptable to

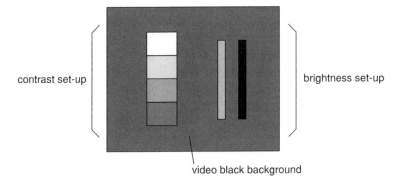

contrast set-up

brightness set-up

video black background

Figure 12.1 PLUGE picture set-up.

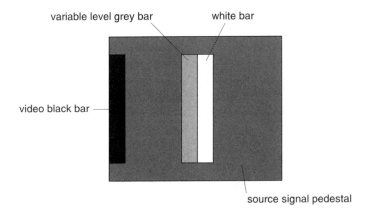

variable level grey bar

white bar

video black bar

source signal pedestal

Figure 12.2 Vical picture set-up.

the varying conditions found on location and offers brightness and contrast adjustment that fits the monitor's capability.

Colour

Measuring the light emitted by the CRT phosphors (or whatever method the display uses) is best carried out by using a proprietary method, although an experienced eye should not be ruled out. Black balance is carried out first followed by white balance. For the procedure relevant to a particular display, follow the manufacturer's instructions.

Using the picture

Despite the eye's inherent unreliability it can function as a measurement tool. It does so because it is sensitive to difference. Difference of tone or shades of colour when displayed side by side are very easily discerned. The eye fails where long-term memory is required; it cannot carry absolute values. However, when pictures are shown in succession the eye will reveal colour and luminosity differences. Final camera checks must always use the picture. The eye and the picture will quickly show how well cameras match.

Even more critical is to sit a person in front of the cameras and study flesh tone differences from camera to camera. Subtleties will be revealed that are beyond conventional test and measurement.

Measuring with Vical

Vical was designed as a portable measurement and reference unit for location composite monitoring, and makes use of the principle of comparison. The monitoring signal passes through Vical and, in doing so, a calibrated grey bar of variable level is inserted into it. Using the picture, the camera white balance can be checked by comparing the inserted grey bar to the grey card as reproduced by the camera. The instrument has the facility to remove colour to make the luminance match possible, then by restoring the colour, any remaining colour balance error is revealed. Likewise, a black balance check can also be carried out. Camera pedestal may be measured by the same method. Vical also serves as a useful grey reference in picture as in Figure 12.3 for location or fixed installations.

Figure 12.3   Measuring with Vical. Here Vical is used as a spot meter. The level of the grey bar is adjusted to match the skin tone. The read-out shows what level the bar has been adjusted to. Therefore, in this example, the skin tone measures almost 60%. Compare with Figure 12.4.

Vical is a picture-based system; it cannot carry out engineering functions such as measurement of syncs or timing. But throughout this book, stress has been placed on the importance of pictures and their relationship to the WFM. The Vical in-picture measurement method is an alternative to using waveforms. Too much reliance on the waveform in operational situations can lead to what may be described as 'picture blindness', where the individual fails to trust their own eyes and turns therefore to the WFM for decisions which are of a pictorial nature.

The in-picture waveform

A growing alternative to the traditional WFM is to turn the picture monitor into a waveform display. Modern digital processing makes possible signal analysis, then re-processing to present it to the picture monitor as a picture of a waveform. Such instruments have many of the facilities of conventional WFMs and at the same time offer a size and cost advantage, the display being, of course, already provided. A portable example is shown in Figure 12.4.

Figure 12.4 In-picture waveform. The advantage of in-picture waveform and vector displays is that the display size may be as large as the picture, or, as here, waveform and vectors shown side by side. Showing the picture at the same time is also most useful. Versatile waveform and vector monitoring in a compact battery-operated instrument is of particular value in location and remote situations. Using waveforms and vectors display for actual pictures is of limited value. However, the fact that here the signal has exceeded 100% may be very important.

In-picture measurement has developed beyond the portable WFM and vector display to more comprehensive test and measurement demanded by digital video and audio in permanent installations. Making use of existing picture monitoring offers great space and heat savings in a complex modern video suite.

CHAPTER 13

MORE ON PICTURES

The Good Picture

Goodness and badness are illusory when we venture into the esoteric world of picture making. No parameters, no rulers, no waveforms; the subjective cannot be subjected to the conventions of measurement. Yet we often hear remarks such as, 'Aren't the pictures good …' Or bad, middling, nice, pretty. Who can measure prettiness? We can only measure what we can touch, take hold of, do things to. And now a huge shift has taken place; the centre of gravity has moved. Video has lifted picture making out of the exclusive preserve of the professional. Now, it is the consumer in the driving seat, with digital and wide screen, PC editing, and all the bells and whistles of the big screen. And there we have the paradox … the expectations have gone askew. The man in the street has all of these but what of the rest … that which makes for good craft—good pictures? A tripod? The latest 'How to Make a Movie' book? Why do we still see him shooting like he's got a pistol or a hose pipe? Well, the camera's got anti-wobble technology, hasn't it? The consumer's driving the technology. Is this the Good Picture?

Screen appeal

One of the most significant developments has been the picture display. But were it not for a gadget right at the beginning of the chain, improvements to the picture wouldn't have been worth the consideration. This was, of course, the DVD (digital versatile disc). Essentially a ROM (read only memory), but to the viewer—the film goer—this simple plastic disc the size of a man's hand, brought cinema into the living room. Now, it is films for everyone: buy, rent, and slip in the pocket and out into the machine. And it is film at its highest quality—higher than the average show print, and as cheap as a couple of seats to see that said same print in the local cinema. It really is home cinema, and the viewer expects—and gets—everything: wide screen, full tonal range, full colour, full sound that goes right the way round, and everything in perfect clarity. No weave, no dirt, scratches or grain, no missed projector changes, not even those nasty, splashy cue dots. Perfect telecine transfers of the original or re-mastered prints, and we see for the first time, the way it was photographed ... there's nothing but digits between cinematographer and viewer ... Let's relax and enjoy the movie. But hold on ... where does this leave measurement?

Contrast and gamma, and beyond

It all began, as this book began, with the CRT. The cathode ray tube, having set the standard of video pictures for over half a century, is bowing out at last. Its very bulk, weight and power requirements, not to mention the hazard of a large glass-enclosed vacuum, will soon relegate it to the museum. New technology is moving in to take its place: LCD, plasma and projection, and there may be, and probably are, more. The trend now is toward larger displays, clearer and brighter images brought by digital video, not to mention high definition. But the CRT will leave a legacy that will hang around for some while yet ...

It was the CRT that determined the parameters for colour, dynamic range and tonal gradation—constraints that at the time had to be accepted and worked around. The current television system reflects this. For instance, both gamma (tonal gradation) and contrast range (dynamic range), arise out of the characteristics of the cathode ray tube. The corrections for these were made in the camera, a sufferance that arguably held up camera development in earlier years. Refer to the Appendix for the background to these parameters, and also to Chapter 7 and the camera set-up procedure.

Contrast range was determined by the signal space available to terrestrial TV transmission. The CRT dictated how bright the picture would be. Black was as low as transmission noise would allow. Basic conditions indeed. The contrast range at best was 30:1. This was pretty paltry when compared to film, which easily reached 1000:1 and more. When we realise that modern 10 bit digital video works out about the same, it's easy to see the sudden surge of interest in the picture. What point is there creating, sending and being able to receive perfect pictures if the means to view them are denied us? It's easy to heap all the blame on the CRT. A very great deal hung on the viewer, and it was only when that lone voice eventually came to be heard—that better pictures would sell more programming—that things began to move on. The tube, once an integral part of a carefully crafted system, is now becoming more of an anachronism every day.

Of the improvements sought from better screens, contrast was first on the list: blacker blacks and brighter whites. The cinema followed the orthodoxy of theatre: films were shown in the dark, unlike TV where this was considered pedantic. Even the best of television drama suffered the ignomiy of 'kitchen viewing'. Meanwhile, in the cinema, the seated audience enjoyed a large screen. Projection, film or electronic, requires a reflective white screen: the more reflective, the brighter the picture. A good solid black, therefore, means good solid blackout. Modern electronic projectors claim contrast ranges of the order of 1000:1 and more, and this fits well with 10 bit digital video and DVD.

Measuring the screen

Screens fall into two main types: light generator, such as CRT and plasma, and reflective, the ubiquitous white screen. It is an inevitable fact of life that all of these will perform differently, yet at the same time will have characteristics that are measurable.

Light output measurements are specified under ideal conditions, which are usually laboratory conditions, but this need not preclude carrying out a simple procedure of one's own. In fact it's important to do so. Displays not only differ, they change with use. Measure any display after a year's use and dirt and misalignment will easily reduce a contrast range of 1000:1 to 500:1 or less, not to mention changes in colour rendition. The message here is regular and reliable servicing. The gamma issue still applies. What should viewing gamma be? The CRT dictates that the video signal is pre-gamma corrected (see Appendix), and therefore all other displays, cinema or home cinema, theatre projectors, plasma and LCD, should follow this standard. Wherever video, standard or high definition, analogue or digital, is the source material, it must be gamma corrected. Which means that the new displays must have the CRT characteristic *built in*. If not, the picture will be tonally distorted. A similar constraint also applies to colour rendition.

Measuring the screen is not so onerous as at first seems. In fact, such diversity of picture displays and viewing arrangements, not to mention the near limitless control now available, makes screen measurement a worthwhile procedure for any picture maker. The requirements are a light meter and test signal generator and a darkened environment. Naturally, it is assumed that the display—monitor or projector—is aligned as per manufacturers' instruction before you begin. And this, of course, is the other side of the issue … good handbooks and good engineering. But let us assume for the moment that all is as it should be. We may well find out that it isn't but that's all part of the exercise.

Regardless of the display type, allow it time to warm up, say, half an hour. While it does so we can go over the procedure. We are going to feed a signal of known level without colour, i.e. grey, to the screen, and the light it produces will be measured. The object is to ascertain the relationship of signal input to light output. The test gear is simple: the author uses Vical (see Chapter 12), as it has a calibrated grey bar of variable level. Although functioning only in composite video, many displays have composite inputs that will accept NTSC or PAL, and this is perfectly valid for this test. However, any generator of variable level grey will do. If necessary use a WFM to measure the level. The light meter used is a Pentax Spotmeter IV. Note that this is the analogue version; the later digital one seems unable to cope with the display refresh rate, and reads spuriously. Another point to note—a very important one—is never, NEVER place a standard needle-type instrument of the exposure meter kind onto the screen of a CRT. The magnetic field will instantly magnetise the internal mask to such a degree that the tube's own degauss system may not be able to clear it. Standard light meters are designed to operate at a distance from the subject, and it is inadvisable to bring them closer than needed. A spotmeter allows readings to be taken at normal viewing distance. Endeavour to restrict measurement to the central area of the screen, at least avoid the edges and corners.

The procedure is as follows:

- Set the test signal to 100%, or white level.
- Measure the light output from the screen. This is the brightest the screen has to deliver and will be the reference for the test.
- Reduce the test signal level until the light meter reading falls by 1 stop. Note the level of the test signal.
- Continue reducing the test signal, noting the level at which the light output falls by each successive light stop. Continue right down to as close to black as possible.
- Normalise the signal to a scale of 0 to 1.0, e.g. 50% = 0.5. The light readings are stop values: each stop less is halving the light output. Therefore, setting the highest at 1.0, the next will be 0.5, the next 0.25, and so on as far as the resolution of your readings will permit.
- Draw a graph of signal input to light output, extrapolating back to the axis origins of zero signal and zero light.

The result should be similar to that in Figure A.1 of the Appendix. Variations will be inevitable but the basic shape of the curve should be evident.

Figure 13.1 compares a typical CRT to an LCD projector, but note that here the signal input axis at the bottom is in logarithmic form, which would result, theoretically, in a straight line.

For the test shown in Figure 13.1, the CRT monitor chosen was a small (14 inches, 36 cm) one, of some years old, but it was of a 'black screen' type. That is, the screen had a black appearance, giving a greater tonal depth but at the expense of overall light output. The test illustrates very well how video monitoring can be compromised in high ambient light. Using a monitor—any monitor – under conditions where ambient light is so high that it compresses effective contrast range will compromise performance. Should the contrast be raised to compensate, the tube will overload and compress further the tonal range. Nor will errors be confined to CRT-based displays: all types are vulnerable to overload.

High definition and other digital systems not able to use the above procedure for screen measurement have an alternative. It involves producing

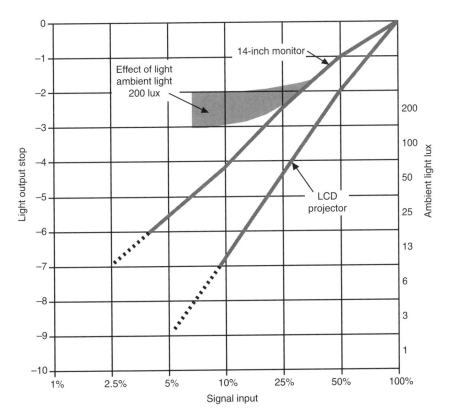

Figure 13.1   Contrast and dynamic range: projector versus CRT. Light output against signal input of a Sony LCD projector as used in a medium-sized theatre, and a typical 14-inch CRT monitor. Note how closely the LCD follows the ideal straight line, while the CRT has a marked flattening above 50% signal level as the light output is unable to match signal input. Scaled down the right-hand side is ambient light. At 200 lux (daylight or bright indoor light), the effect is to degrade the useful contrast range of the monitor to between 2 and 3 stops (the spread of the curve is due to variations across the screen of reflected light). The dotted lower sections of the plots are where accurate measurement is compromised. But note how the projector aims toward a signal level of about 3–5%, a residual 'lift' due to light spillage and leakage.

a source of grey on a PC with a suitable proprietary software, say Photoshop®, and transferring to digital tape, hard disc, DVD, or even sending over a network. The test signal could be a greyscale of as many steps as convenient, from black up to white, the level of each step being known. Experiment to get the best result—check the levels of the final video version with a WFM. Keep a copy as your own standard to measure screens whenever there's the need to do so.

A picture line-up test signal such as PLUGE (see Chapter 12) can also be used. However, the all-important portion near black is not well catered for, as the difference between levels is too large. It would also be as well to check these with a WFM. There are also proprietary picture set-up techniques aimed at the home cinema—a good indicator of the value now placed on domestic film viewing. One example, by Video Essentials, is called 'Optimizing Your Audio & Video System'. Although aimed at the consumer, it is very comprehensive, extensive and thorough, and, being available on DVD, is very convenient.

Screen types

New picture displays currently emerging onto the consumer market use LCD and plasma screens. Both are flat panel, light weight, and lower power consumption than the CRT. Of the two, the plasma shows most similarity to the current wide screen CRT; both are available in 32 and 42 inches (82 and 107 cm) sizes. For tonal range, sharpness and brightness, the two match each other very well. They also exhibit similar frame flicker, something not apparent with the LCD screen. In fact, the LCD screen exhibits smoother motion … not very 'movie-like', but some find it a restful picture to watch. An LCD screen does not overload in the same way as a CRT. The liquid crystal elements are not light generators, but controllers, varying the amount of transmitted light. The brightness of the image depends on the power of the back light, typically a fluorescent tube. Earlier liquid crystal screens were very directional and off-axis viewing had unpredictable shifts in colour saturation and tonal gradation. More recent versions have largely eliminated this effect.

A plasma screen, being a light generator, would be expected to show similar overload constraints as the CRT. As with the CRT, high ambient light levels would incline the viewer to raise contrast and brightness to compensate with the inevitable overload as the screen reaches its maximum output. How significant this might be, how better (or worse) than a CRT, only time and user experience will tell. This is not to say the LCD is immune to ambient light: the screen is only as bright as its backlight. But the effect is different; increasing the backlight to compensate does not suffer the same limitations as driving pixel-based light emitters. Figure 13.2 illustrates this. Practical issues, however, arise. In the white areas of the picture all the light is transmitted, but in the darker ones the screen must either absorb or reflect the unused light. This unused energy has to go somewhere, and it is getting rid of the resulting generated heat that imposes limitations. Used in full sunlight the lamp power would be considerable, placing unacceptable demands upon the screen. Hence, an LCD screen may also require shading.

An example of a high-power back light is the LCD projector, where the power of the projector is based purely on the power of the lamp.

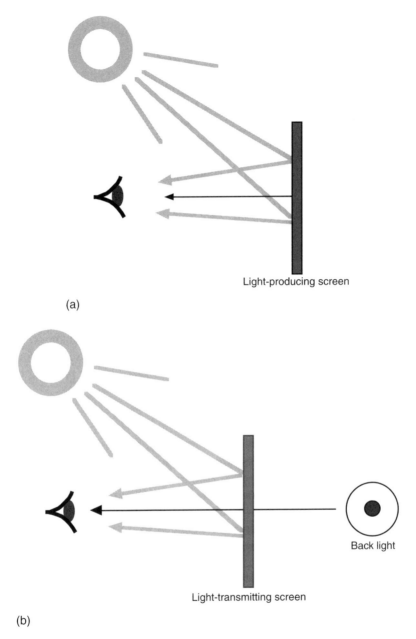

(a)

(b)

Figure 13.2   Screen light versus ambient light. (a) Typical light-emitting screen, CRT or plasma. The screen has to generate sufficient light to compete with ambient. As the screen reaches maximum light output, tonal values become more compressed and eventually limit. (b) A back-lit screen is theoretically able to compete with ambient light without distortion. The lamp power is adjusted until the picture is as bright as required, i.e. whites should match the brightness of a piece of white paper placed alongside, but there are practical limits as to how powerful the back light can be.

about viewing in daylight. While 10 bit digital provides 10 stops, daylight viewing crushes this down to the good old fashioned 5 stops, less if the TV is perched on the kitchen window sill.

What about high definition? For cinema, theatre, home cinema, we're relaxed and at ease: a glass of wine and the lights off … and HD hits us just where it counts: the Wow Factor, and isn't it good to see pictures as they were intended. High definition is getting established with a standard of its own. HDCAM uses 1080 vertical pixels and 1920 horizontal, and can be either interlaced or progressive. Progressive scan is like film: a complete frame at a time. The options include a 24 frames per second rate (24P) to make the result even more film-like.

High definition, or just standard digital, the reasoning is the same. If we have these large dynamic ranges to play with, we can re-adopt the exposure meter because it allows us to cast off the role of 'lighter' and take up that of 'cinematographer': to think more about pictures. Look at how the light plays, windows and camera angles, decide highlights and shadow. See them, measure them. Within 10 stops? Go over the essential elements of your picture. Do they fit into the system? They do? Then set the camera to expose for them. Go back to the monitor and see the effect. And what you see —if you've measured correctly—is your light range accommodated where and how you want it. The meter allows you to work as film. Think as film. A good monitor is the best of video—if it's used properly. Used together, the best of video and the best of film can produce formidable results.

Figure 13.3 illustrates scene contrast and camera contrast. In the next chapter we see how the same logic applies to audio … and has the same pitfalls. Signal space, regardless of how large, has limits for which due regard must become second nature.

Now, as video assumes its rightful place alongside film, we can apply the film philosophy further. Take out of the camera all that is thought of as 'video': gamma, sharpening, and colorimetry. Let the light hit the sensors, straight into digital, and be recorded without hindrance. Do all the rest later: gamma correct—let's give it a different name: call it 'tonal balance'— and colour too. In the warm and comfort of post production, with no artist time to worry about, or that threatened change in the weather. The luxury of 'try it and see'. This is right back to where film began. It's where HD is heading. But beware though of how your material will be viewed. No longer can we rely on the display because a DVD can play in anywhere, and that means video …

How big is the picture?

This has now become part of the aspect ratio issue, and it's all tied in with viewing distance. Some years ago a study of viewing distances was

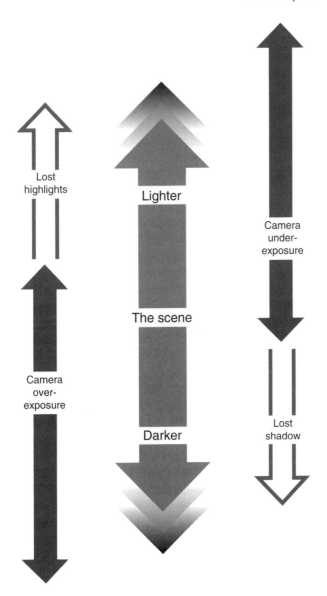

Figure 13.3　Fitting the picture into the system. Outdoor scenes invariably have a contrast range exceeding that available to the photographer. Decide on essential highlights and shadow and expose the camera to ensure these are accommodated. To misjudge exposure is to throw away valuable signal space. Refer back to Chapter 4 and Figure 4.1.

carried out based on the subjective evaluation of four 'qualities' of picture (David Wood, Diffusion EBU, Spring 1995). These were defined as HDTV (high definition TV); EDTV (enhanced definition, or highest quality); SDTV (standard definition TV); and LDTV (low definition, typically a domestic video recorder). The yardstick was picture *height*, not width. The results were:

HDTV	ideal viewing distance	3 × picture height
EDTV	ideal viewing distance	4 × picture height
SDTV	ideal viewing distance	6 × picture height
LDTV	ideal viewing distance	9 × picture height

There may have been slight changes to categorisation but essentially the figures still hold true. And by using height the question of aspect ratio—the width of the picture—becomes irrelevant.

The original TV aspect ratio of 4 × 3 (1.33:1) is now being overtaken by what has become known as 'wide screen'. The standard wide screen format for video and television is 16 × 9 (1.78:1). The film world has over a number of years created many aspect ratios but it is not the intention to go into all of these.

And as far as measurement goes, aspect ratio doesn't really alter the situation. There may be changes to the information rate—if the camera has a 16 × 9 sensor, and is shooting wide screen, then more information will be created than if it were only 4 × 3, assuming the same image height and resolution. Some cameras, now mainly restricted to low-end and domestic, are 4 × 3 and achieve wide screen by using only the central band of the sensor. Thus, vertical resolution is reduced, which could mean slipping from, say, EDTV to SDTV. Not quite what wide screen is about.

A story of lost colour

Look at the rainbow and you'll see all the colours of colour bars. Look at the inside of the bow—inside blue, which we're told is the shortest wavelength of all. So what colour is shorter wavelength than blue? It's an odd one: sometimes called indigo. Indeed, an odd one because it is beyond blue, and therefore should be outside the range of our eyes. It's certainly beyond our cameras. However, the human eye can see it … a bit of our far distant heritage still lurking there. To many insects it's absolutely brilliant. This is the near-ultra violet, and many natural colours, particularly flowers such as bluebells, respond vividly to ultra violet.

We see the effect of UV additives in clothes washed with the 'whiter-than-white' additive, which works by reacting with the UV in sunlight. The theatre uses UV lamps to produce ghostly effects with specially coated costumes, props or décor. Modern discharge lights often produce sufficient UV to react with the clothes' washing additive, so much so that a white hankie used to white balance a camera may give a yellow balance because to the camera the hankie appears more blue than white.

But that colour indigo is a colour too far for video. It slips around the colour analysis. That's why so many purples and pinks that look to the eye so wonderful appear quite dull and lifeless on screen. Similarly, lighting design using discharge lamps filtered to produce indigoes and purples can also be very disappointing.

The bad picture

All that we have discussed revolves around one thing... and it's not measurement. It's understanding. Measurement is only part of the business of understanding the whole. More and more we find newcomers to the industry ill-equipped to deal with aspects of the craft once taken for granted. The basics—of which measurement is one—slide into the morass of confusion surrounding the technical to be ignored and left to someone else. But who? A trusty technical? Someone who knows nothing outside their bailiwick of technology is not encouraged to know, has no interest there? Of course it may be argued that the technology has become so sophisticated as to make much of what has been discussed earlier in this book impracticable or unnecessary. But to ignore, to assume that all is well, is to risk. To understand better what goes on inside boxes, behind lenses, is to give that edge when the unexpected happens. When the expected fails to materialise because technology has been allowed to step in front, to make decisions for us. That's the bad picture.

Another scenario. The bad picture is someone else's fault. Was it really someone else's ignorance that screwed up the best picture you'd ever shot? If so, tell them. Explain to them why and how it could be put right. Listen to their answer; consider their position. The problem isn't just yours; it isn't just theirs. It belongs to everyone. Yet do those of us who possess the experience and knowledge have a duty to inform? Do others have a duty to listen? Nothing need hinder the free interchange of knowledge: it requires only a will to do so.

We are led to believe that this sophisticated technology will do anything: we are told by those who should know and don't, and by those who do know and should know better. If we meet technology face to face, understand it and accept it for what it is—a tool—then it will do good work for us. Make the good picture.

CHAPTER 14

INTRODUCING AUDIO

Sound and audio refer, of course, to one and the same thing, but it is worthwhile clearing up a little semantics confusion between sound levels and programme levels. Sound is a generic term more applicable to the acoustic, whereas audio is a signal and often referred to in the UK as *programme*.

As far as measurement goes, audio has similar constraints to video—namely, headroom and noise. Between the two exists the signal space available for recording and transmission.

Considering the noise limit first. This is where the signal becomes so quiet as to be lost in the electrical clutter that we call *noise*. Developments over years have steadily pushed the noise floor farther and farther down. Low-noise amplifiers, noise cancelling, compression, noise reduction, as well as the steady improvement in signal generation, have improved substantially signal-to-noise ratios. Historically, audio signal generators, such as microphones, gramophone pick-ups, and tape replay heads, produce low-level signals. The high-gain amplifiers used to raise these levels to usable values must generate as little noise as possible. Amplifiers amplify whatever appears at their inputs, so noise has to be dealt with right from the very first point of the system.

Headroom imposes a maximum signal level. In video white level is maximum. White is an absolute, but the equivalent in audio terms is much harder to define. Traditionally, it was the maximum power a transmitter would deliver, but since the introduction of recording, it is the recording medium that became the limiting factor. These are overload constraints which, if not adhered to cause at very least distortion, at worst actual damage. Other limitations have also become increasingly relevant. Examples are loudspeakers, particularly in these days of high sound levels, and—very importantly—sound pressures on the ear. But it is essentially transmitters and tape that have brought about the need for audio signal measurement.

In earlier chapters of this book audio was used as an aid in the understanding of video. Now, having established the latter, we can return to audio with—it is hoped—greater confidence. As sensors, both the eye and the ear have that super-intelligent signal processor, the brain. Both, therefore, possess similar attributes. They are able to accept signals over a very large dynamic range, to cope with changes in the environment, allowing us the uncanny genius to concentrate on what we want and to exclude that that we don't want. These attributes are ever-present, they must be recognised and accepted, made allowances for, and ultimately turned to the advantage of the programme maker. Sound and pictures must work together. One will always endeavour to 'come in front of the other'. It's quite natural that this should be. Our attention will unconsciously shift from picture to sound track throughout the programme, as each takes its turn in the story telling. We make use of this: the way pictures are cut together, how sound is laid over. By the same token it may also conceal: perception blanking is where flaws pass unnoticed because effects elsewhere take our attention. Indeed, good pictures have been quoted as an excuse for bad audio: thankfully, not often.

Although, where our senses are concerned, pictures and sound are very similar, it is when they are converted into signals that real differences emerge. And this, in the main, is largely down to our collective education and experience. We readily accept a picture created on a screen by the skill of the photographer, yet require a sound track that is as pure and natural as possible. Of course, this is an overly simplistic view—each demands creativity in its own right—but it does serve to illustrate how our ears and eyes have driven audio and video along their respective paths of development.

One fundamental difference is bandwidth, a technical issue that we discussed in Chapter 2. The other, a less recognised one, is dynamic range, the signal space required for accurate sound reproduction.

Video is based on a dynamic range of 30 to 1, and although later developments have pushed this much further, as we saw in the previous chapter, it still falls far short of that required by audio which must be at least 1000 to 1. One might be forgiven for thinking that with so huge a range, measurement would be impracticable, some might go so far as to think it unnecessary. After all, a scale calibrated over such a huge range would be most ungainly. But the numbers are misleading. The ear cannot distinguish changes of volume to the degree of accuracy that a scale of 1 to 1000 implies. In fact the average human ear can barely discern a change by a factor of 2 of acoustic power: that is a halving or doubling. Hence the use of the logarithmic decibel (dB) scale (see Appendix) that relates signal levels to perceived *changes* in sound volume. Now, a dynamic range of 1000:1 corresponds to 60 dB. You may say these are still ungainly figures, but good sound reproduction needs all of this space to convey the naturalism we require. In fact, by modern standards, 60 dB is not now considered sufficient, and 100 dB has become the accepted standard. 100 dB corresponds to a dynamic range of 100 000 to 1.

Let's think more about decibels. This is expressing differences, or changes, of signal level (see Appendix). A change of 3 dB is a doubling or halving of signal *power*, which, as has been stated above, is only just discernible to the ear. Power is directly related to signal level, and 3 dB is a change in level, or voltage, by a factor of 1.4. Distinguish between *power* and *level* with care. Level is a voltage (or current) in a circuit, a cable, feeding a loudspeaker, sent to a recorder. Power is the product of voltage and current

Preceding programme with line-up, or zero level, tone is standard procedure, as it is with colour bars. And yes …it's well known, this doesn't always
happen. But without a reference how is the destination to know where to
set the received level? Do you wait for a sudden peak to hit red, or wonder
at length why the programme's so quiet? A situation that applies equally to
off-tape, from a server, at the end of a line, down a satellite link.

But where do we actually place line-up level in the signal space?
Traditionally, it is 12 dB below onset of distortion, and that's at PPM 4,
or −4 dB on a VU meter. Referring to Figure 14.1, and the scaling of a PPM
in 4 dB steps (above PPM 2), we can see that +12 dB occurs at PPM 7.
This is the point of overload. Therefore, PPM 6, at +8 dB above line-up, is
usually accepted as the operational maximum, and allows a further 4 dB of
headroom to accommodate transients. PPM 4 is therefore line-up; PPM 7
is absolute max. This is a standard world-wide, but as already mentioned,
local variations do exist, so it's worth checking beforehand.

Whatever the system or standard, line-up level should always be adhered
to. If, for instance, a recording is made at too low a level, we throw away
signal space. To compensate, replay gain will be increased which will result in
lifting of the ever-present noise floor. If this be done at the end of the chain—
say, by the listener at home raising the volume of the wireless or player—the

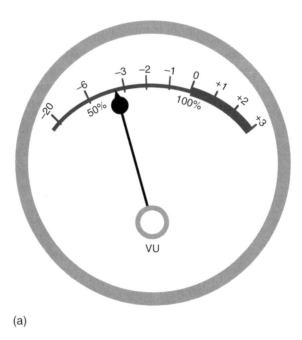

(a)

Figure 14.1a VU and PPM. (a) Older-style VU meters have a percentage
scale for transmitter modulation. (b) The PPM has a scale of 1 to 7 in 4 dB
steps, except 1 to 2, which is 6 dB. (c) The standard line-up level for tone is
PPM 4 and VU −4dB, although variations do occur.

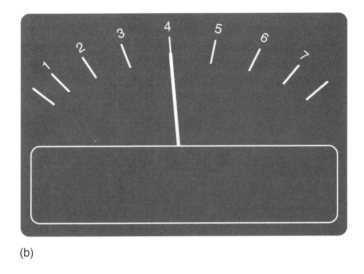

(b)

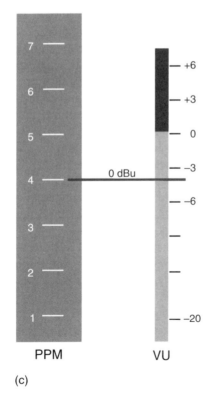

(c)

Figure 14.1b,c   (continued) VU and PPM.

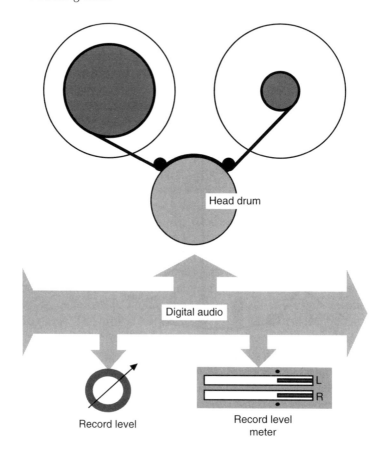

Figure 14.3 Digital audio tape. The record level and metering act in the digital domain. The digital audio passes through the machine from input to output on a data bus. Metering, record level and the tape itself access the bus. A recorder that accepts an analogue signal may use a conventional analogue level, or gain, control. In a studio, the input level may be set by the mixer or desk, as described for analogue line-up.

Figure 14.4 compares the dynamic ranges, analogue to digital, but bear in mind that these are idealised figures. The audio CD is also 16 bit, as is the MiniDisc®. DVD-Audio, the new audio format based on the DVD, has a number of options up to a 24 bit, and is similar to top-line professional recorders with a dynamic range of 140 dB.

In practice much depends on how the system is used as to how good digital audio actually is.

Try a simple test. This is to ascertain the maximum a digital recorder will accept, and is applicable from the most basic recorder upwards.

Using line-up tone, you're going to increase the signal to the recorder until the point of overload is heard. But before doing so, spare a moment to think of loudspeakers and ears: your own and other people's. Keep listening

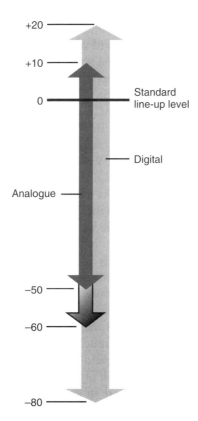

+20

+10

0 — Standard line-up level

— Digital

Analogue —

−50

−60

−80

Figure 14.4   Analogue versus digital tape. Analogue and digital dynamic ranges compared. Note that the analogue range of 60 dB can be extended by noise reduction techniques to around 70 dB. The principle of noise reduction is based on the *compander*: the incoming audio is *compressed* to raise the level of quieter passages above the tape noise, and then *expanded* on replay, therefore reducing the noise. There are many variants, analogue and digital, that have been developed for a range of uses.

volumes down. Also, watch out for metering; if this is mechanical it may be overloaded too. As the recorded level rises, so the replay level should be reduced. A sudden harshening of the replay output indicates the maximum has been exceeded, and record level should be brought down until just below that point. Note the meter reading as you rock the recorder input level; the onset of distortion should be as the record meter goes into the 'red'. Note how a dB either way makes all the difference. The irony is, to the average ear, one decibel is virtually indiscernible.

A good all-round guide is to set your line-up level for zero-level tone at 20 dB below the maximum you have just determined. This is referred to as −20 dBFS (dB full-scale), but again, be mindful of local standards. This is the level at which you will record line-up tone at the start of each programme tape, or send down the line to destinations, and is a very useful 8 dB better

distance is invariably fixed to suit the picture, the microphone may have to make do with being too far from the subject. Noise from lens and tape transport of seemingly very quiet camcorders can be an unexpected problem, particularly when auto record stretches out its legs during those precious moments of silence. Position the camera for the best picture, and put out a separate microphone for best audio.

Audio connectors

Unbalanced cables, or circuits, are prone to noise pick-up due to one of the conductors, the outer screen or sheath, being connected to earth or equipment frame. Professional audio invariably uses balanced interconnections between equipment. Film and video studios are potentially electrically noisy places due to lighting rigs. In the field, where there is no control over power supply, this may be 'dirty' for a variety of reasons.

A balanced circuit has two conductors, or cores, usually twisted together, and surrounded by, but not connected to, the copper sheath. Distinguishing which conductor is which might be thought immaterial: by definition a balanced circuit means that they are identical and therefore interchangeable. While reversing them will not impair the performance of the circuit, it will reverse phase. For example, two microphones, one with reversed phase, and close enough to pick up the same sound, will produce signals that will be 180 degrees out of phase. When mixed together these signals will cancel. In stereo operation phasing is absolutely essential. The conductors are therefore coded white and red, and often annotated Hi and Lo.

The most common audio connector is the XLR 3-pole, which carries one audio circuit in balanced form.

The jack is the other common connector, mostly used as a jackfield interconnect. This is a co-axial connector of 0.25 inch (6.4 mm) diameter; the centre pole, or tip, is surrounded by a ring, and a sleeve which forms the body. There are two types, with differing tip and ring dimensions. The professional type has a tip and ring of smaller diameter than the sleeve, and is plain brass. Other variants of the jack, mainly for domestic use, are two-pole unbalanced, three-pole stereo and also in smaller sizes. See the Appendix for more detail on connectors.

In the UK, the cores of balanced cable are (in most instances) colour coded white and red, which correspond to Hi and Lo. Beware of mixing cables made for other countries and organisations, as this could result in phase reversal.

A further variant of balanced cable is four cores with screen. Known sometimes as star-quad, this further reduces the chance of noise pick-up, and is used where audio and lighting cables cannot be kept apart. The cores are wired as pairs in parallel: that is, opposite cores are connected together, forming the equivalent of two conductors of the balanced pair.

Stereo signals are coded left and right, A and B, red and green, respectively, in professional systems. Domestic stereo, however, uses white and red as left and right. These differences must be considered when, as often happens, domestic and professional systems are used alongside each other. It is convention to consider the left, or A, channel to be the master channel. Adjustments are therefore made to the right, or B, channel for matching purposes.

In multicore cables, colour coding will usually be determined by the equipment manufacturer. Digital audio is often encoded with its video counterpart in the video environment, sent and received as part of the SDI interface in coaxial cable.

Sound levels

We cannot leave audio without mentioning the health and safety aspect of acoustic sound levels. Measurement here has become a straightforward procedure, easily carried out, and an essential one. High sound levels are not the exclusivity of rock concerts: noise can create an issue anywhere, from a drama shoot in a factory, to a symphony concert. Exposure time, proximity, how enclosed the work area is and the type of sound, all influence the outcome. Standard metering is readily available, and detailed instructions about how to use should be on hand. A figure of 90 dBA (this is sound pressure) is generally regarded as the upper limit for an 8-hour exposure. However, both measurement method and permitted levels vary, so check local conditions and regulations.

A big question hangs over headphones. How does one measure sound level on the actual eardrum? So much depends on the air-coupling diaphragm to eardrum, the fit of the ear pads, shape of head, whether there's a 'filter' of hair between the two. One may be forgiven for arguing that it is user responsibility. But is the user acting under instructions? Where does the liability rest then? This is where measurement provides no answer. One can only advise caution.

At the beginning everything might work well. Until one day the return video quality suddenly worsens. Why? The bookings are the same: digital send; analogue return.

The reason is simple. The circuits' contractor has upgraded all the routeing centres to digital. However, if you book an analogue circuit, that was what you get. But no one actually explained that at each router the signal was converted from analogue to digital then back again. That was where the quality had gone: repeated conversions. Conversion is where the signal is at its most vulnerable. Convert at the very beginning, convert back at the very end, and don't do it in between.

Here's another conversion predicament. Once upon a time aspect ratio was 4×3 and all was happy in the land. Then came wide screen. Many viewers, however, remain old fashioned, which means their TV sets are still 4×3. The TV station has to decide who to please: the old folks or the wide boys. Producers specify which format to have their programmes made in, and most, naturally, choose wide screen. In a please-all executive decision the pictures get converted to 14×9 for transmission. Then for a late night re-edit of the highlights we're treated to 16×9. But from which material? The original or the 14×9? And, yes … it's sometimes the latter. Now the material has gone through two conversions. All digital, of course, but there's cropping for one, expanding for the next. It's not unknown for a picture that began life with a healthy 500 or 600 lines of resolution to end up with a miserly 400: a sad loss indeed.

Domestic bliss

Re-writable CD and DVD have blossomed. Everything, it seems, can be put onto a plastic disc. But not all of them are quite so easily played. Not all players acknowledge the presence of a re-writable; some refuse to 'see' the material recorded there. This is a compatibility issue, and one that is as complex as the secrecy surrounding the various formats and subs of formats.

But it's here that the lowly domestic player has a role to play. Most of the so-called low-end machines are designed to cope with the variable quality of material that gets thrown at them. They play when their high-end siblings often won't. The message is, don't discard a disc as unplayable before trying it in other players (and don't ignore CD and DVD computer drives either). The cheapest one of all may save the day.

Brain teasers

Page 27. The timed sequence. How bandwidth is affected by changing the rate of information transmission. Recording the event and playing back the tape at twice the speed means that all the frequencies on the tape appear doubled. Doubling the lowest (the 25 Hz frame rate) won't impact on bandwidth, but the highest at 5 MHz will. This will appear at 10 Mhz. So bandwidth requirement is doubled.

Page 36. Calculating the bandwidth requirement of a 50 frames per second system. Using the example on *page 31*, doubling the frame rate from 25 to 50 per second requires that each line must be completed in 32 µs, thus effectively doubling the bandwidth requirement to 13 MHz. Halving the number of lines restores the line length to 64 µs, and the bandwidth returns to 6.5 MHz. A bandwidth of 3.25 MHz transmitting 25 frames per second would have half the picture resolution as that of 6.5 MHz. The picture would therefore appear less sharp. Or to retain the same resolution, the frame rate would have to be 12.5 per second.

Page 44. When a battery is applied to the input of a WFM the trace will disappear. The clue on the label is the battery voltage: almost certainly more than the 1 volt of video the WFM is designed to display. Therefore, the trace will have moved right up and disappeared out of the top of the screen. If the battery is exhausted it will read lower, of course, and the trace may reappear. An extra note here about WFM triggering: some instruments will not display unless video is present. External triggering provides a way around this, so read on through Chapter 4, paying particular attention to Figure 4.14.

Page 123. The Cb blue component has somehow got delayed. This will show as a blue fringe to the right of picture highlights, or if more serious, a complete shift of the blue image to the right. The left-hand edges will show the complimentary yellow fringing.

Page 161. Why is this *obviously* an analogue fault? The shape is the clue. This is a component signal, both the luminance and red components are the correct shape, but the red component is distorted. It has lost its sharp, rectangular shape, and the result would be red/cyan smearing across the picture. This fault arises due to a faulty Cr circuit; it could be a damaged cable. If a digital signal suffered a similar fault it would apply to the other components as well, and it may fail entirely.

AND FINALLY...

We must never forget that at the end of the chain we view an analogue image and hear analogue audio. That is how we function. This is the medium of communication, and must be understood in its own right. It's a human creation and technology, whether analogue, digital or any other form yet to be invented, must not be allowed to take control over it.

We must at times step back and consider the effects of our actions. We must take time to consider the whole, how we affect others in their work, how they affect us, and why.

The business of broadcasting is experiencing a proliferation of standards and offshoots of standards: a situation brought about by protectionism and commercial interests that often restricts the sharing of not only technology, but of understanding. Development is not always carried out *for* the consumer but in the *name* of the consumer. At the bottom line, the standard engineered so carefully is continually under threat for it is seen by some as a hindrance.

The theme of this book has been the standard. And the standard, after all, is no more than a mere tool of our work. Understanding the whole system is vital if quality is not to be subjugated by other interests.

And when all is said, what remains is only a book. No panacea lies within these pages, only principles.

APPENDIX

A.1. Gamma

Gamma in television is a feature of the cathode ray picture tube. The CRT is based on the triode thermionic valve, which has an inherent non-linearity. Picture tube gamma causes compression at low signal inputs and expansion at high signal inputs, and results in the exaggeration of tonal difference dark to light. The relationship of normalised input to output is:

$$Input^\gamma = output$$

For a CRT, the gamma is 2.2, and is defined as:

$$Input^{2.2} = output$$

This figure is fairly consistent but some variation occurs mainly from design differences and ageing. The transfer characteristic of a standard picture tube is set out in Figure A.1. A gamma of unity is shown as a dashed line for comparison.

Black-and-white television benefited from tonal compression near black for it reduced the detrimental effects of noise. However, gamma compression causes colour saturation errors. Correcting a gamma of 2.2 requires the opposite gamma of 0.4545. It was decided to make gamma correction as early as possible (to retain the better noise performance): that is, at the camera. Pre-distortion at source to correct an error at the destination means the signal chain is 'gamma corrected'. All picture sources must, therefore, have a gamma of 0.4545 and all picture displays must have a gamma of 2.2 (whether CRT-based or not). The relationship of light input to camera, to light output of the screen should be linear, i.e. an overall gamma of unity.

Gamma correction is shown in Figure A.2. In practice, the correction is modified for circuitry design reasons. Theory requires that correction begins at black with a gain of infinity, which is an impossibility. In practice, the initial gain is limited to 5 up to a signal output of 20%. From 20% the curve follows a gamma of 0.4. This approximation has been adopted as a standard. Camera manufacturers have interpreted gamma correction in slightly different ways. Some industrial cameras use an initial gain of 3.5

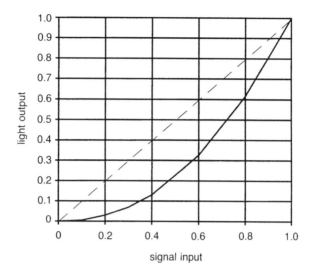

Figure A.1   Picture tube gamma characteristic.

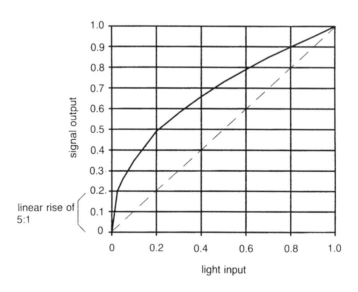

Figure A.2   Camera gamma characteristics.

giving a slight increase in dark tone density rather similar to raising gamma to 0.45 in a broadcast camera.

Although a gamma of 0.4 is now a broadcast standard, lighting directors and photographers, seeking greater creative control, alter camera gamma to suit their own specific purposes as already described.

Table A.1 Camera light input and signal output relationship

Light input		Signal output
100%	(90% reflectance white card)	100% (clip level)
50%	−1 stop	75%
25%	−2 stops	55%
18%	(18% reflectance grey card)	50%
12.5%	−3 stops	40%
6.25%	−4 stops	25%
3.125%	−5 stops	3% (pedestal level)

A.2. Contrast range

This defines the scene tonal range of the video system, usually as applied to cameras. The input/output relationship of a typical camera is set out in Table A.1 and shows the non-linearity of gamma correction. From this can be seen that the contrast range of the camera is five stops, where one stop is equivalent to doubling or halving the light input. The camera lens is calibrated in stops. At black (or pedestal) the signal becomes lost in system noise; as noise figures improve so effective contrast range increases. But, it must be remembered that to appreciate any extension of the contrast range, the picture display and viewing conditions must be upgraded accordingly. See Chapter 13 for more information.

Extending contrast range by compressing higher tones, as with the 'knee' characteristic (see DCC in Chapter 7) is less dependent on viewing conditions. Using lower gamma has a similar, but not identical, effect whilst a higher gamma does the reverse.

Raising pedestal also reduces contrast range. For instance, by raising to 10% the useful signal range will occupy only 90% of the available system contrast range.

A.3. Gain and signal levels

Gain, or amplification, expresses the increase or decrease in signal level, or amplitude. Gain is specified in decibels (see Appendix A.4) or as a factor. It may also appear, when related to light levels, as light stops. NTSC and PAL have been taken, for the purpose of this book, as having the same signal values. The actual values are as set out in Figures A.3 and A.4.

Decibels, dBs	−6	0	6	9	12	18
Gain (factor)	$\times\frac{1}{2}$	$\times 1$	$\times 2$	$\times 3$	$\times 4$	$\times 8$
Sensitivity (f-stops)	−1	0	+1	$+1\frac{1}{2}$	+2	+3

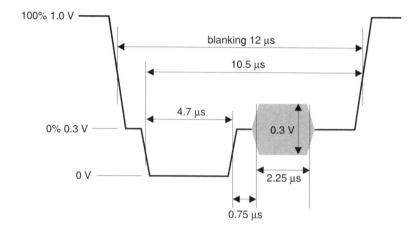

Figure A.3 PAL line sync period.

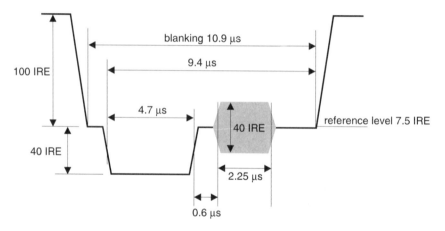

Figure A.4 NSTC line sync period.

A.4. Decibels (dB)

Decibels are a logarithmic function with origins in audio measurement (see Chapter 14). The unit is relative with no absolute value. Therefore, it measures only *changes* in voltage (or current), or *changes* of power. Audio measurement uses line-up level of 1 mW in 600 Ω, and this is a datum given the value of zero and the notation dBu. Values higher than 0 dBu are positive; those below are negative. Where the decibel is used for acoustic, or sound pressure level the notation is dBA. Decibels may be derived from voltage (or current) changes, or from power changes. The relationship is:

$$\text{Decibels} = 20 \times \text{log of change of voltage (or current)}$$
$$= 10 \times \text{log. of change of power}$$

The table gives some typical values:

-60	-20	-6	-3	0	$+3$	$+6$	$+12$	dB
0.001	0.1	0.5	0.7	0	1.4	2	4	factor of voltage change
10^{-6}	0.01	0.25	0.5	0	2	4	16	factor of power change

A.5. Standard signal values

PAL is by convention, measured in volts. NTSC is in IRE values, which are based on percentage of maximum picture. Note that the NTSC and PAL amplitudes differ slightly. NTSC white is 100 IRE, which is 714 mV (0.714 V) above black. NTSC sync is at 40 IRE below black, which is 286 mV (0.286 V). This slightly larger picture-to-sync ratio (the total signal remains at 1.0 V overall) is to offset the effect of NTSC fixed pedestal of 7.5 IRE. Fixed pedestal is now no longer a requirement of the 525/60 line digital component video standard (see Figures A.3 and A.4).

Field sync is a sequence of half line frequency pulses known as the broad pulses because of their length. Equalising pulses are the half line pulses either side of the field sync that ensure the field sync is in the same relative position in every field (see Figures A.5 and A.6).

Some of the unused blank lines after the field sync may be used for ITS (insertion test signal), video tape timecode, identification and other information.

A.6. Light measurement

Light power is measured in the SI unit, candelas, or the imperial unit, candle power. The light leaving a light source to illuminate a surface area is measured in lumens. The illumination of one candle power at one foot is one foot-candle, or one lumen/sq. foot and is the standard imperial unit of illumination. The metric equivalent is the lumen/m^2, or lux.

Therefore,

$$1 \text{ foot candle} = 1 \text{ lumen/ft}^2 = 10.76 \text{ lux}$$

Light meters (or exposure meters) are usually calibrated in foot candles or lux, sometimes both. Typical studio light levels are 80 foot-candles, 860 lux. Modern cameras can work down to 10 lux and lower, but such light levels are not practical for normal studio operations.

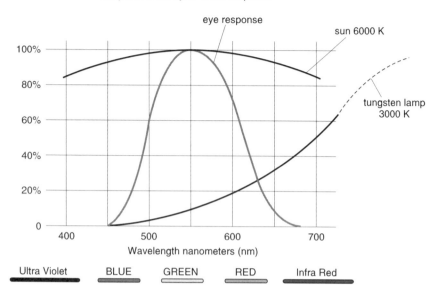

Radiation from the sun and tungsten at normal operating temperature compared to the eye's colour response

Figure A.7   Relative spectral response. Radiation from the sun and tungsten at normal operating temperature compared to the eye's colour response.

A.7. Colour temperature

This is the relationship of light colour to temperature. An object, on being raised in temperature, emits radiation. At first this is only heat but as the temperature rises so the object begins to glow. Heat is infrared radiation, which is invisible to the human eye. As temperature rises the radiation is at first red, then orange, then yellow; finally it reaches white heat as it approaches the sun's surface temperature at 6000 K. Everything radiates heat; it is only at absolute zero—zero Kelvin (−273. 15°C)—that radiation ceases.

At 3000 K tungsten glows orange/yellow. The eye continually balances colour to normalise, similar to the camera white balancing, and is generally unaware of the colour differences between tungsten lighting and daylight (Figure A.7). Tungsten lighting is flexible because it is easily varied in brightness. It does, at the same time, alter colour for the reasons set out above. Operating a tungsten lamp about 80% output gives useful adjustment either side, giving a typical colour temperature of 2900 K and much longer lamp life than when worked at full output.

Colour temperature may be adjusted by light filtration, either at the camera, or the lamp. Correction filters from tungsten to daylight, 3000 K to 6000 K, and daylight to tungsten are commonly available, as are intermediate values for fine adjustments to match lamp colours.

A.8. Colorimetry

The science of colour. The principle of additive colour as used in television is based on numerical colour values applied to the primaries, red, green and blue. The unit of light is the lumen and any colour may be defined as:

$$n(C) \equiv x(R) + y(G) + z(B) \quad \text{where n, x, y and z are in lumens}$$

The standard CRT phosphors defined for television deliver 0.3 lumens of red, 0.59 lumens of green and 0.11 lumens of blue, to produce 1.0 lumen of white. These are normalised to equal values such that:

1 unit of R + 1 unit of G + 1 unit of B $\equiv$ 1 unit of white

Hence, the equal values RGB used by the video standard. The conversion factors from lumens to equal values is introduced in the camera, the reverse taking place at the screen. Once equal values are in place, it is easy to define any colour and its luminosity by matching it with specific values of the three primaries. A colour may be seen as specified by the coordinates X and Y. These are derived from the CIE (Commission Internationale d'Eclairage, the international commission for illumination) colour diagram. Further reading is recommended for a more complete understanding of the subject.

A.9. Termination

A video circuit consists of a source driving a destination via a cable. The source has a resistance of 75 ohms and the destination terminates with a load of 75 ohms. These are specified as resistors. The cable has a characteristic impedance of 75 ohms; impedance is the combination of resistance and reactive (capacitive and/or inductive) elements (see Figure A.8). Current driven by the source voltage travels around the circuit through both 75 ohm resistors. Each resistor dissipates half the circuit power; therefore half is lost at the source and half received at the destination. But because the cable source and termination requirements are met, there is minimal cable loss and distortion.

Digital video (SDI) requires closer tolerances regarding cable characteristic and termination in order to minimise bit errors.

A.10. DC restoration

It is not possible in a practical video circuit to maintain direct current transfer (DC), which is an essential feature of the signal. The input circuit in

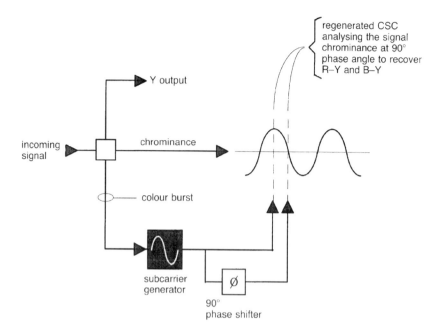

Figure A.12   Principle of colour decoding. The incoming signal is split into subcarrier, Y, and colour burst. The colour burst is used to lock the decoder's oscillator to regenerate two outputs of CSC, one phase shifted to 90°. These 'look for' subcarrier in the signal, and, where present, recover the colour difference signals.

The carrier offers protection to the colour signal against interference and distortion. However, interference between subcarrier and fine scene detail, e.g. patterns in clothing and scenery, gives rise to 'cross colour', interference patterns. Hence, where possible, the Y and C signals are kept separate, as in S-VHS recording and the high density picture monitoring found in many digital studios.

Figure A.12 is a simplified overview of the decoding process. This requires that regenerated CSC is locked and synchronous to the incoming colour burst. Colour burst is created in the encoder as part of the colour difference signals and is therefore modulated onto the CSC in exactly the same way as scene colour.

PAL differs from NTSC in its 'swinging V axis'. The subcarrier for the V modulator passes through an inverter every other line; therefore, burst and V chrominance switch polarity together (the integrity of burst to chrominance phase relationship is upheld). Interlace means that adjacent lines are from alternate fields. With PAL switching applied, alternate fields have alternate V subcarrier polarity. Hue errors on successive lines will therefore appear in opposite directions; the eye is unable to differentiate between lines

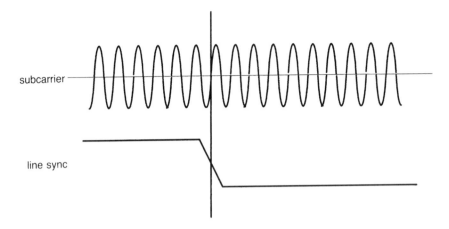

Figure A.13 SC-H phase. The standard states that the leading edge of line sync must be coincident with the positive going subcarrier. The diagram shows the line sync leading edge and subcarrier magnified. After 4 fields (2 frames) the subcarrier is back in phase with the start of field 1. NTSC is therefore a 4-field sequence.

and the error will pass unnoticed. More sophisticated electronic cancelling is applied with 'delay PAL'.

A.12. SC-H phase

Subcarrier-horizontal phase, also known as 'colour framing'. In composite video, chrominance and luminance are not independent of each other. Subcarrier, PAL: 4.43361875 MHz, NTSC: 3.579545 MHz, is the master signal and from it is derived the line frequency, PAL: 15.625 kHz, NTSC: 15.734 kHz. Field rates are determined by the number of lines and length of line. They are 50 Hz in PAL and 59.94 Hz in NTSC. Therefore, all elements of the timebase are related. If the frequency of subcarrier changes, the line and field rate change accordingly, so retaining the time and phase relationships within the signal. Chrominance and luminance cannot be separated and rejoined without due consideration of subcarrier phase and line timing. The relationship is known as 'SC-H phase'. The specification states the subcarrier phase-to-line timing relationship and is set out in Figure A.13. Chapter 9 mentioned the PAL 4-frame sequence, and Figure A.14 describes what SC-H phase means to the NTSC system.

The differences in field rates and the number of lines in the two systems influence choice of subcarrier frequency. NTSC has the least complex SC-H relationship. The number of cycles of subcarrier per NTSC field is:

$$\frac{3\,579\,545 \text{ cycles/s}}{59.94 \text{ fields/s}} \approx 5918.75$$

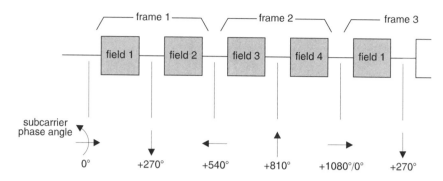

Figure A.14 NTSC colour framing or SC-H phase. During one field, subcarrier does not complete a whole number of cycles, ending with $\frac{3}{4}$ cycle, or 270°. This accumulates until, after field 4, subcarrier phase returns to that at the start of field 1. The process then repeats. After 4 fields (2 frames) the subcarrier is back in phase with the start of field 1. NTSC is therefore a four-field sequence.

The '0.75' after the decimal point is three-quarters of a cycle, or 270°, which means that over one field, the subcarrier does not complete a whole number, as described in Figure A.14.

Colour framing in PAL is twice as complex. PAL subcarrier is 4.43361875 MHz, giving:

$$\frac{4\ 433\ 618.75\ \text{cycles/s}}{50.00\ \text{fields/s}} = 88\ 672.375\ \text{cycles/field}$$

An odd number of quarter cycles is indicated by the '0.375' and results in the PAL colour framing having an 8-field sequence. That is, four frames before subcarrier phase returns to its starting point.

In studios, SC-H phase is dealt with as part of the sync pulse generation system and all picture generators will be locked together maintaining the appropriate field sequence. Video tape is less predictable because of editing. Each tape player must be aligned to its neighbour in the 4 or 8 field sequence. Should non-consecutive fields of the sequence be edited together, the sub-carrier phase will jump over the edit, causing a brief colour change or slight shift sideways shift of the picture.

SC-H phase may be considered insignificant; a cycle of subcarrier is only one-twentieth of the duration of line sync. The frequency of subcarrier was decided upon when black and white TV was well established and compatibility was of prime interest. Subcarrier would be visible on black and white receivers as a dot structure and both standards came up with different answers to reduce this. Field rate, number of lines, and, in the case of PAL, the alternating colour phase, all influenced the final design outcome.

As part of the composite standard SC-H cannot be ignored. When breaking PAL or NTSC signals down into their components for any kind of manipulation and re-assembling again, SC-H has to be borne in mind. To ignore it is to run the risk of an automatic checking system finding an error and rejecting the signal.

Measurement of SC-H phase is not straightforward; the time scales of subcarrier and lines and fields are too great to display on a WFM. It is therefore necessary to use a special technique, of which a number have been developed over the years.

A.13. Audio connectors

The standard audio connector is the XLR-3, which has three poles, or pins. The cable is a twisted pair, or two-core, with outer copper braid, or screen. The signal is carried by the twisted pair in balanced format (i.e. the signal flows forward and backward equally in both conductors). The screen acts solely as shielding and earthing (grounding or bonding) between equipment frames. The standard UK pin allocation is 1 – screen, 2 – signal Hi (red), 3 – signal Lo (white). Note that the colour code may vary. Note also that connections to pins 1 and 2 are reversed in some organisations and countries.

Jack connections are tip – signal Hi (white), ring – signal Lo (red), sleeve – screen. These connections apply to both 1/4 inch (6.4 mm) and miniature jacks.

The DIN may be used for microphones. Pin allocation is 1 – Hi, 2 – screen, 3 – Lo. Other types of connector may be found on equipment. Check handbooks.

Other nomenclature in common usage: Hi – hot, Lo – cold, earth – ground.

GLOSSARY

Italics refer to index or other glossary entries.

AC	Alternating current. Electric current that changes direction of flow. See *sine wave* and *DC*.
Aliasing	Interference effects between parts of the signal with common features.
Amp	The standard unit of electric current. See *voltage*.
Amplifier	A device to increase signal level. To do so requires the supply of power. See *Proc Amp*.
Amplitude	Amount of signal. See *level* and Index.
Aspect ratio	The ratio of picture width to height. See Index.
B & B	Black and burst (sync and colour burst).
Bandwidth	See Index.
Bar graph	A linear thermometer-like electronic display of audio signal level.
Battery	A source of electrical energy held in chemical form. Also used to denote a battery of electric cells. See *power supply*.
Binary	See Index.
Bit	Binary digit. 0 or 1.
BNC	The standard video bayonet locking coaxial connector.
Breezeway	Portion of the video signal between trailing edge of *line sync* and start of colour burst. See Index *back porch*.
Broad pulses	The *field sync* pulse sequence. See Index.
BS	Black and sync (sync only, picture at black).
Byte	Digital number or word. A *bit* sequence.
Cable	Wire-based circuit.
Capacitor	An electric component. Holder of an electric charge. A capacitor has an insulator that stops the passage of *DC*. *AC* flow increases as its frequency rises. See *inductor*.
CBS	Colour, black and sync (sync and colour burst).
CCD	Charge coupled device. A silicon pixel array onto which the image is focused so building up an equivalent electric charge that is read off to form the video signal.

Charge	An electric quantity that is not flowing.
Circuit	What an electric current flows in. See *transmission circuit* and *circuitry* and Index.
Circuitry	The electronic circuits inside equipment. See *circuit*.
Coaxial	Two-wire cable where one conductor is totally enclosed by the other, known as inner and outer (or screen). Also coaxial connector, see *BNC*.
Colour black	Black and burst. See Index.
Compression	Reducing signal bandwidth or memory requirements by sending only essential information, e.g. only sending picture movement information.
Configure	To construct, or set up, a system to perform a particular task. See *jackfield*.
Conforming	Where source play-in material is edited down to a finished programme.
Connector	The means of connecting cable to apparatus, etc.
CRC	Cyclic Redundancy Check. See Index.
CSC	Colour subcarrier. See Index.
Current	The movement of electricity. Current only exists when a *voltage* is present to drive it around a *circuit*.
CVBS	Colour, video, black and sync (complete composite video).
DAT	Digital Audio Tape.
dB	Abbreviation of *decibel*.
dBa	Decibel unit for audio, now largely superseded by dBu.
dBA	Standard decibel unit for acoustic sound pressure measurement.
dBFS	dB Full Scale. Decibel unit for digital audio recording, based on maximum available bit count.
dBm	Decibel unit now superseded by dBu.
dBu	Standard decibel unit for audio. See Appendix.
DC	Direct current. *Current* flow that is constant and does not change direction. See *AC*.
Decibel	Logarithmic unit of voltage, current or power difference, or change. See Appendix.

$$dB = 20[\log \text{ (voltage, or current, difference)}]$$
$$= 10[\log \text{ (power difference)}]$$

DVD	Digital Versatile Disc, similar to CDROM, but having 4.7GB (gigabytes) of memory space. A number of versions of the format exist. The standard domestic media for TV programmes and feature films. A high definition (HD) version is proposed.
DVD-A	DVD-Audio. One of the DVD family, similar to audio CD but with higher capacity. See Index.

Dynamic range	See Index
EBU	European Broadcasting Union.
EDH	Error Detection and Handling. See Index.
EQ	Abbreviation of equalisation
Equalising pulse	The pulses occurring either side of the *field sync*.
Gain	Increase (or decrease) of signal level expressed as a factor, or in *decibels*, that is achieved by a *circuit*, *amplifier*, or other piece of equipment.
Genlock	The method of video *synchronising* by slaving one piece of equipment to another. See Index.
Gigabyte	1 Gb. One thousand megabytes (strictly, 1024 megabytes). See *byte*.
HD	High definition (video)
HDTV	High definition TV
HDCAM	High definition recording standard. See Index.
Horizontal sync	Another name for *line sync*.
Impedance	The control of an electric *current* by *resistance* and *reactance* separately or combined. The term is used whenever a circuit is not pure resistance.
Inductor	The opposite of *capacitor*. The inductor passes direct *current* but opposes changes of current flow. *AC* flow increases as its frequency falls. See *capacitor*.
Insulator	Stops the flow of electric current. May be described as infinite resistance.
IRE	Institute of Radio Engineers. 'Percentage Unit' of signal level, or 1/140th of 1 V.
ITS	Insertion test signal. A test signal inserted into the *field blanking* period.
Jackfield	The means of interconnecting sources and destinations, apparatus and circuits. Enables system interchange or re-configuration. See *configure*.
Kilobyte	1 Kb. One thousand bytes (strictly 1024 bytes). See *byte*.
LCD	Liquid Crystal Display. A compact and low power image display that works by changing its light transmission with applied voltage.
Level	Amount of signal, normally stated as voltage, occasionally as power. See *amplitude* and Index.
Line	Alternative term to *circuit* but more usually denoting a cable-based circuit.
Line rate	The frequency of the video picture line structure.
Megabyte	1Mb. One million bytes (strictly 1024 kilobytes). See *byte*.
Memory	The electronic storage of information.
Microprocessor	Digital calculation or manipulation chip.

Microsecond	One millionth of a second.
Millisecond	One thousandth of a second.
MiniDisc®	Miniature digital audio recorder developed for the domestic market, uses removable optical disc.
Monochrome	See Index.
MPEG	Motion Picture Experts Group, an industry standards setting body. A video compression standard.
Musa	Standard coaxial slide-fit connector as used on *jack fields*, longer than the *BNC* but smaller diameter.
Nanosecond	One thousand millionth of a second.
NTSC	National Television Systems Committee. The 525 line, 30 (strictly 29.97) frame/s analogue composite video standard for broadcast television in America, Japan, etc.
Ohm	See Index.
Oscillator	A generator of alternating signals, usually sine wave, but not necessarily so.
Oscilloscope	See Index.
PAL	Phase Alternate Line. The 625 line, 25 frame/s analogue composite video standard for broadcast television in Western Europe except France, Russia, etc.
Phase	Measure of *synchronism*, or signal coincidence. Relative timing of signals or sine waves.
Power	The amount of energy transferred in a given time. Product of *voltage* and *current* and measured in watts. See also *decibels*.
Power supply	Source of electric power as supplied to equipment. See *Battery*.
PPM	Peak Programme Meter. See Index
Proc amp	Processing amplifier. In video systems it restores synchronising pulses and colour burst to their correct shape and position. Provides black level, gain and peak white clipping adjustment.
Ramp signal	See Index.
Raster	The scanning structure of a video picture.
Reactance	The current controlling effect provided by a *capacitor* or *inductor*.
Resistance	The current controlling effect offered by a *resistor*, cable or wire. Measured in ohms its effect applies equally to *AC* and *DC*. See *ohm*.
Resistor	An electric component that is used to provide resistance to current flow.
RGB	Red, green and blue (as separate circuits). See Index.

BIBLIOGRAPHY

Craig, M. (1991 and 1994) *Television Measurements*. Tektronix Inc.

D'Amato, P. (1984) *Study of the Effects of Various Impairments on the 20T Pulse*. European Broadcasting Union.

Gressman, R. (1978) *Guiding Principles for the Design of Television Waveform Monitors*. European Broadcasting Union.

Henderson, H. (1964) *Colorimetry*. Engineering Training Department, BBC.

Hodges, P. (1993) Vical. A Video Calibration System Using a Standard Picture Monitor. *The Journal of Photographic Science*, **41**, p. 21.

Hodges, P. (1994) *The Video Camera Operator's Handbook*. Butterworth-Heinemann, Oxford.

Horowitz, P. and Hill, W. (1989) *The Art of Electronics*. Cambridge University Press, Cambridge.

Rumsey, F. and McCormack, T. (2002) *Sound & Recording: an Introduction*. Focal Press, Oxford.

Sims, H. V. (1968) *The Principles of PAL Colour Television*. Engineering Training Department, BBC/Iliffe.

Talbot-Smith, M. (2003) *Sound Engineer's Pocket Book*. Focal Press, Oxford.

Watkinson, J. (1994) *An Introduction to Digital Video*. Butterworth-Heinemann, Oxford.

Wheeler, P. (2003) *High Definition and 24P Cinematography*. Focal Press, Oxford.

Wood, D. (1995) *Diffusion EBU*, Spring 1995, The European Broadcasting Union.

INDEX